The CEO Factory

Praise for the Book

'*The CEO Factory* is a step-by-step guide to building a great consumer-driven organization. In particular, the sections on creating an organization of "entrepreneur professionals" and using marketing to deeply understand consumers and build a brand resonated deeply with me.'

Binny Bansal, Founder, Flipkart

'HUL to an outsider is full of contradictions – promotions for instance are given only after completing a certain number of years of service and yet professionals are entrepreneurial. Its organizational values endure in the face of erratic economic cycles. This book provides rare insights into the ingredients at HUL that sculpted the few hundred CEOs that came out of it.'

Errol D'Souza, Director, Indian Institute of Management Ahmedabad

'A great insight into how and why HUL is such a fantastic developer of talent – not only for India, but for the whole of Unilever.'

Alan Jope, CEO, Unilever

'HUL has consistently produced world-class talent who have gone on to lead a number of companies in India and abroad. At Airtel, we have warmly embraced senior talent from HUL and a very large number of leadership positions in the Airtel Management Board and in the operating units come from the

HUL stock. Gopal Vittal, MD & CEO of Bharti Airtel Ltd, is one of the galaxy of leaders having cut their teeth and been nurtured at HUL.'

'There are very few businesses in India that are run successfully for a long period with integrity and rigour. Hindustan Unilever is one of them. *The CEO Factory* helps you understand how you can win and be honest. Or perhaps win because you are honest.'

'An MBA in a book ... This book is as much from Sudhir's heart as it is from his head. Drawing on his rich experience during his career, he shares the blueprint on how HUL builds brands and businesses by adhering to principles and by a constant understanding of the changing needs of the consumer.'

The CEO Factory

Management Lessons
from Hindustan Unilever

Sudhir Sitapati

JUGGERNAUT BOOKS
KS House, 118 Shahpur Jat, New Delhi 110049, India

First published by Juggernaut Books 2019

10 9 8 7 6 5 4 3 2 1

P-ISBN: 978-93-5345-084-7
E-ISBN: 978-93-5345-085-4

Typeset in Adobe Caslon Pro by R. Ajith Kumar, Noida

Printed and bound at Thomson Press India Ltd

To my grandfather V. Ramanathan
who insisted on taking charge of my education when he saw
my father insist on almost nothing
and
To my father, S. Ganesh
The only thing he ever insisted on was that I join
Hindustan Unilever

Contents

Preface

The Hindustan Unilever Story

Few Indians have heard of Hindustan Unilever Limited (HUL). But they are intimate with the brands it sells. To name a few: Lifebuoy, Dove, Clinic Plus, Ponds, Lakmé, Closeup, Surf Excel, Vim, Brooke Bond, Bru, Kwality Wall's, Kissan and, as of 2020, Horlicks. Nine out of ten Indian households use an HUL product every month. Forget Google and Facebook, more Indians use HUL products than those who own a television, those who vote or even those who have running water or electricity. Even if you don't know much about Hindustan Unilever, you have grown up with it and you are touching it every single day of your life. Just like your parents, grandparents and their grandparents.

While researching for this book, I came across a faded copy of the first annual report of the newly incorporated

Hindustan Lever in 1958. The company was already among the largest in the country and made a profit after tax (PAT) of Rs 1 crore.* In 2019 the company made a profit of Rs 6080 crore – a compound annual growth of 15 per cent. In the same period that HUL grew its profits 6000 times, the Indian economy grew 1400 times. It is hard to find another large company that has delivered 15 per cent earnings growth over sixty years anywhere in the world. It is nearly impossible to find one that has stayed in the top five of a large country for over sixty years.

It is not just the long-term performance of HUL that is stellar. Its current return on capital employed (ROCE) of 92 per cent is by far the highest in the country. In just the last decade it has given shareholders an annual return of 23 per cent with its stock price up seven times.

This has made HUL an iconic company on Dalal Street. If analysts were to rate Indian companies over a century on financial and non-financial impact, HUL would feature on the top three of all and number one of most lists. HUL's market cap has now crossed $60 billion, making it one of the most valuable fast moving consumer goods (FMCG) companies in the world, ahead of the global valuations of Colgate Palmolive, Kraft Heinz, Mondelēz and Reckitt Benckiser.

---

* 1 crore = 10 million; Rs 70 = US $1 (approximately)

Apart from being omnipresent in our lives and being at the top of the business game for a very long time, HUL is an enormously influential company. For the last decade HUL has been ranked by AC Nielsen as the Dream Employer of Choice in the top twenty business schools in India. HUL is taken extremely seriously in government circles with many of its past chairmen being Padma Bhushan and Padma Vibhushan awardees. Most famously, nobody gives more CEOs to corporate India than HUL. From Nestlé to Diageo to Airtel to Hindalco to DMart to Raymond to the Star Network, there are currently around 400 HUL alumni who are CEOs/CXOs across corporate India. In corporate circles HUL is well known by the nickname 'The CEO Factory'. Because of the influence of its alumni many business practices in corporate India have their origin in HUL. This is obviously the case in sales, marketing and HR, but it also exists in finance, supply chain, R&D and legal. There is a good chance that not only are you using HUL products, you are already working in a way that HUL does.

This book asks and then answers the question of why a company this large has been successful for so long. What exactly do managers learn in HUL that makes them so much in demand as CEOs across industry?

A lot of people assume that there must be a codified HUL way of doing things that its managers are able to apply elsewhere. Well, there isn't. Plenty of internal rulebooks exist, but the real HUL way resides not in manuals but in practices and beliefs. There is an HUL way of advertising, of sales and of running a manufacturing operation. These are well-defined processes. There is also an HUL way of operating a business: with rigour, consumer connectedness, discipline and above all integrity.

I joined HUL in 1999 as a management trainee. During my twenty years in the company, I have worked across the three divisions in HUL – Personal Care, Home Care and Foods and Refreshments – in a variety of roles and am currently also an Executive Director on its Management Committee, getting a bird's-eye view of the entire organization.

I draw from these twenty years of experience to try to synthesize how I think HUL works, warts and all. But it is like the story of the blind men describing an elephant. Despite the time I have spent here, I can only infer from my own subjective experience. I hope the many HUL employees and alumni who have seen other sides of this elephant will be motivated to write down their own views.

It is also a perilous job writing a book like this while still serving the company as an Executive Director. What should one keep confidential? How honest can one be about the failings of the company? How extensive should I be in giving credit to the people who have contributed to company wins? My former boss Sanjay Dube reminded me that my primary responsibility in writing this book is to the reader and with the exception of genuinely confidential information this is the principle I have tried to follow. Needless to say, the views expressed in this book are entirely my own and not of HUL.

The first chapter deals with the characteristics that have made HUL a CEO factory. Chapters two to eight look at different functions within HUL and how they work: from marketing and advertising to sales and cost management and HR. Chapter nine concludes with the values that have been drilled into generations of HUL managers.

I hope this book is useful to corporate executives trying to understand how HUL thinks about a function like advertising or cost management; to entrepreneurs trying to build a culture in their organization; to MBA students trying to get a broader-brush view of the corporate world; but most importantly to anyone in India trying to build an institution that lasts.

Let me start with a few lines on the history of HUL and how it came into being. If you believe, as Henry Ford did, that 'history is bunk', you can skip it and go to the first chapter directly.

Behind HUL: English Marketing, Dutch Acumen and Indian Entrepreneurship

Hindustan Unilever is a child of two parents: the British Lever Brothers and the Dutch Margarine Union merged to create Unilever in 1930. But 'Hindustan' Unilever has the unique mix of this European Unilever with a special Indian twist to its DNA, having adapted to Indian conditions for the last six decades. Let us begin with the birth.

William Lever, the founder of Lever Brothers, was an enlightened, if eccentric, capitalist. Joining his father's grocery business, he soon spotted the opportunity for pre-packed goods. He created a washing soap that was different from other soaps in the market as it contained none of the fillers or chemicals that added to the size of the soap but did nothing for its performance. He set up a company, naming it Lever Brothers and the product Sunlight. Sunlight was smaller but contained more punch than other soaps, and in a few years, by 1888, it had become one of the biggest brands in the United Kingdom.

Lever Brothers soon began to face competition from an unlikely source. Margarine, a butter substitute made from vegetable fat, was discovered in 1869 during the Franco-Prussian war when butter was in short supply. The invention of hydrogenation (increasing the melting point of oils through the addition of hydrogen) allowed the making of margarine from cheaper vegetable oils. This brought the Dutch margarine makers Margarine Union in direct competition with Lever Brothers, who used vegetable oils in soap, for the sourcing of vegetable oils.

Both considered a merger. Apart from competition for raw materials, there was another strategic reason for the merger. Margarine Union was on a financially stronger footing but was essentially a continental European company. Lever Brothers on the other hand had a wide global footprint but had lately been in financial difficulties because of over-expansion by its colourful founder. This mutually beneficial merger between the Dutch Margarine Union and the English **Lever** Brothers resulted in the creation of Unilever in 1930.

Two of William Lever's exceptional qualities continue to be part of HUL's genetic pool: brilliant marketing and social responsibility.

A salesperson in his early days, William Lever had an instinct for marketing. Lever was by no means the pioneer in advertising. That credit probably goes to Pears soap's (incidentally, now owned by HUL) Thomas Barrett. His somewhat meaningless catchphrase 'Good morning, have you used Pears soap' became so popular that in the early twentieth century no 'top-hat-doffing was complete without the greeting', says Adam Macqueen in his must-read *The King of Sunlight* (a definitive biography of William Lever).

Lever however transformed advertising from mere name recognition to product benefits being conveyed in an insightful manner. An early ad of Sunlight, for instance, shows a woman doing back-breaking laundry, and its caption reads 'Wonder why a woman looks older sooner than a man'. A famous Persil detergent ad from a later period chuckles to the photo of two girls in differently white uniforms 'Someone's mum isn't using Persil'.

But if William Lever is remembered today, it is mainly in his role of the enlightened capitalist. In 1888 near the soap factory at Warrington, he built a town called Port Sunlight for his employees. At a time when 90 per cent of British citizens did not own their own homes, Lever employees were given free housing, medical care, schools, recreational facilities and, most radically, pensions. Port Sunlight is now recognized as the earliest example of a factory city, the most famous Indian example of which is the Tatas' Jamshedpur.

When it was founded in 1930, Unilever already had its genetic code in place: a Protestant work ethic and commercial acumen from its Dutch owners and brilliant marketing with a strong social conscience from its English founder, William Lever. In the 1950s Unilever chairman Geoffrey Heyworth introduced a third genetic strand, one that differentiates Unilever even today from other multinationals. Heyworth felt that as Unilever expanded globally it needed 'delegation to the end of the limbs'. Overseas units were to be run not by expatriates in London but by locals who were much closer to the market. It was a formal HR policy called 'ization' and the organization to benefit the most was the recently formed Hindustan Lever Ltd.

Birth and Growth of HUL

William Lever introduced Indians to the joy of Sunlight and Lifebuoy as early as 1888, to meet, as he characteristically put it, 'the washing needs of the teeming millions of India'. The precursor companies to HUL, Hindustan Vanaspati Manufacturing and Lever Brothers, were incorporated in the early 1930s. Both were owned by Unilever, though Hindustan Lever Limited (as HUL was formerly known) was formed by their merger only in 1956. So in a sense the real history of HUL in India is over 125 years old.

The history of HUL can broadly be broken up into three phases: a phase of market development followed by managing in a highly regulated environment and then competing in an open economy. Each of the three phases has added to the genetic makeup of HUL: from the importance of category development, to being resilient and innovative in times of extraordinary difficulty to becoming an even more consumer-focused company. If the genes that HUL inherited at birth were Dutch thrift and British marketing savviness and social consciousness, ever-changing Indian conditions have made HUL resilient and innovative. The first phase lasted till the 1960s, where mainly British, but also a few Indian, managers introduced India to the core categories of vanaspati, soap, tea and powder detergent.

A few decades before this, Lipton and Brooke Bond (both part of HUL today) responded to Viceroy Lord Curzon's clarion call to develop the domestic tea market in order to find an outlet for the excess tea production that was taking place in Assam. Tea, a quintessentially British drink, was treated with suspicion in India. It was considered an addiction and something that weakened you. This led to the creation of Indian chai, high in milk and sugar content, that was sold to the customer as a nutritious drink, as the undated ad on p. xxi shows. The invention of 'chai' is just one example of HUL's core management principle: developing new categories.

Nihal Kaviratne, a former chairman of Unilever Indonesia, told me how HUL developed the market for detergent bars. In 1957 HUL launched Surf NSD (non-soapy detergent) powder made from petrochemicals.

Until then Indians had washed their clothes with HUL's Sunlight laundry bar, which was made from vegetable oil. Surf powder was more effective but required a habit change – that of soaking clothes. Remember this was well before washing machines had arrived, and Indians were reluctant to clean clothes (or dishes) by soaking dirty things. To bathe, Indians scrubbed and poured water on to themselves, and would not dream of stepping into a tub.

HUL initiated a gigantic effort to knock on doors and demonstrate to sceptical housewives that solution washing with the NSD product would lead to far superior results. These women were used to direct application, but saw that the Surf powder required much less work: no scrubbing. This was a dramatic improvement for them, since even a good quality soap bar like Sunlight took time to lather in the hard water coming out of their taps. In addition, HUL included plastic buckets as promotional gifts with their new Surf product. Plastic bucket manufacturers made a killing. Surf did make headway, but the majority of Indians, while acknowledging the benefit of an NSD powder, continued to use the direct application soap bar.

B.A. Vatsal had joined HUL as a management trainee in 1964, when he returned to India, cutting short his studies on scholarship at Stanford, to take care of his parents. An outstanding product of Elphinstone College, Vatsal was regarded as one of the finest minds in HUL history and seen as someone with a very bright future. It was he who conceived the idea of providing the housewife with the benefits of NSD in a direct application product. The technical process was convoluted and had not been attempted anywhere else. The English marketing director

(David Webb) was convinced that it was a great step backwards, after the many years of hard work to get housewives to switch over to solution washing.

Vatsal persisted, and pestered Webb, until Webb finally agreed to allow him to market test Rin NSD bar, to prove that it would fail. And so it was that in the late 1960s, a market test was actioned in Bangalore. It proved an outstanding success and the product was launched nationally in 1971. Vatsal passed away prematurely in 1974, but his creation Rin Bar is one of the most famous brands in India today.

The second phase of HUL is from the late 1960s to the early 1980s, when HUL had to reckon with the system of socialist government controls known as the 'licence-permit-quota raj'. While most multinationals either left India or diluted their stake below 50 per cent, HUL persisted. It is not clear exactly why, but it probably had to do with the proactive Indianization of management that Unilever had encouraged in the previous decade.

There were two major challenges HUL faced in this period: price control and Unilever retaining majority control.

Both vanaspati and soaps were subject to price control in the 1960s and 1970s, and in the early 1970s HUL started making cash losses in India. What followed was the adoption of a very Indian entrepreneurial mentality

of flexibility-cum-resourcefulness that persists in the
HUL DNA even today. HUL realized that the imported
oil it was using for soap-making was a drain on India's
foreign exchange reserves, which the government of the
day considered a precious commodity. So HUL scientists
devised soap that substituted locally grown castor oil and
rice bran oil for imported oil. HUL chairman T. Thomas
then went to meet the chemicals minister D.K. Baruah
to request removal of price control in exchange for HUL
saving precious foreign currency. The Congress patrician
told him that nobody used soap, and as evidence claimed
that he himself got massaged with olive oil and a hot
towel every day! Nonetheless, the government agreed to
decontrol soap prices.

Retaining 50 per cent equity share of Unilever was as
tricky. In late 1973 the government introduced the Foreign
Exchange Regulation Act (FERA) where foreign equity
holding would have to be reduced to less than 41 per cent
unless a sector was considered capital-intensive. Since
consumer goods were not considered capital-intensive
the ownership of Unilever would fall from 85 per cent
to 41 per cent. T. Thomas decided to oppose this policy.

In his autobiography, TT, as T. Thomas was better
known, reflected on why he felt it was important for
Unilever to continue retaining 51 per cent share. 'The
first and foremost reason was that I firmly believed in the

Unilever system of developing and promoting professional managers without any involvement of the common Indian failings of linguistic, regional or religious considerations.'

TT did several things to hold on to 51 per cent shareholding. He first offered to export 10 per cent of HUL's turnover to earn the country precious foreign exchange. To meet this undertaking, HUL got into several categories such as chemicals, carpets, leather and fisheries and used its global clout to ensure that the 10 per cent target was met. Second, TT kept negotiating with government for smaller Unilever equity reductions: 85 per cent came down to 65 per cent and then to 51 per cent over several years. He was convinced that government policy would eventually change and it was better to bat through the difficult overs than to give in.

If HUL adapted to government control in the heyday of the licence-quota-permit raj, the early 1990s saw HUL adapting to liberalization. Excise duties fell, consumer incomes started rising and till the late 1990s HUL raked in a bonanza. However, in the new millennium it realized that its tools for competing in a closed economy were blunt in an increasingly competitive India. Local competitors like Nirma were closer to the consumer and big multinationals were willing to forgo short-term profits to get a toehold in the country. The period between 2001 and 2009 was a very tough decade for HUL where share price remained stagnant. In hindsight it was a period where the company strengthened several brands and also unblinkingly defended its laundry business from a major competitor attack. In 2009 HUL had a particularly difficult period on the back of extremely volatile commodity prices. In early 2008 commodity prices led by oil at \$120 a barrel shot up and then crashed in late 2008 to \$40. On the way up, unlike local competitors who just cut media investment, HUL rapidly priced up and on the way down didn't drop prices fast enough. Both decisions cost HUL dearly in terms of market shares. The crisis seems to have got the best back into HUL and since 2010 the company's share price has increased eightfold.

So yes, there is an HUL way of management that insiders and informed outsiders recognize or at least intuitively sense.

Being strongly Indian and simultaneously strongly Western is at the heart of the HUL way of management. The ability to walk the dusty markets while being comfortable in Europe. The inherent belief like William Lever had in being 'Good before being Great'. The Western belief in meritocracy. Dutch economy. Indian entrepreneurship. These pulls from all sides have ensured that HUL has remained successful through the decades.

1

Middle-Class Management
The HUL Way

In 2018 our chairman of thirteen years, Harish Manwani, stepped down. Harish had spent close to forty years in the Unilever system, rising to become global Chief Operating Officer. It was the highest an HUL person had risen. Harish had double-hatted as non-executive chairman of HUL while fulfilling his global responsibilities. He was now finally retiring from the company he loved.

Harish had several farewells and gave many speeches, but he saved his best talk for the retired directors' meet in 2018. The HUL retired directors' meet held every June in Mumbai is among the few HUL alumni events where there are no CEOs. Only those who retired as directors are invited.

It is a unique ritual and I am not aware of any other company that does it. The current chairman shares business progress of the previous year and is then grilled by the men who built HUL. Sharp daggers are unsheathed from dusty scabbards. After the trial by fire, there is a sit-down dinner, drinks and a few speeches by former chairmen and occasionally some others.

At the meet Harish spoke about how unique a company HUL was. What, he asked, was its secret sauce? He gave four answers which you will find woven through this book: a *middle-class soul*, a *meritocratic culture*, managers who are *equally comfortable in dusty Indian villages as they are in London or Rotterdam* and finally *unchanging core values*. These aren't just the ingredients of what makes HUL great, but also the four qualities that make HUL executives such successful CEOs when they run other companies.

Almost every major company in India boasts an HUL man or woman in its top management, and the companies that now have HUL alumni as their CEO include Airtel, Viacom, Diageo, DMart, Star TV, BMW, Raymond and Nestlé. So successful and in demand are HUL alumni in the Indian corporate world that many see it as the ultimate finishing school for the ambitious executive. But it is much more than that. If Harish's four HUL traits are married with the historic demand for HUL CEOs, it means that industry thinks that these very traits are what are required for all companies and, dare I say, institutions that succeed in India.

Everyone I spoke to about the book, including several HUL alumni who have gone on to become CEOs, agreed with Harish's four points. There was however a fifth quality that also came up: the ability of the company to mould its employees into 'entrepreneur professionals', people who followed the processes and rigour required of a professional company but were willing to go the extra mile that only entrepreneurs do.

Let us look at these five characteristics one by one.

A Middle-Class Soul

Like the consumers it talks to, HUL has managed to keep a culture that is quintessentially Indian middle class. Hard-working, frugal, aspiring and humble. Hierarchical, stolid and generally unimaginative.

It starts with the people it recruits: middle-class young men and women who have made it through the gruelling Indian education system. As a consequence, middle-class frugality is built into the company.

I recall travelling with Harish to Delhi when he was COO of Unilever and the keynote speaker at 'Ad Asia', a big advertising industry conference. He refused to be put up in a suite at the Taj and instead the two of us stayed in a comfortable but sober company guest house in Vasant Vihar.

When I joined the company, fresh from IIM Ahmedabad (IIMA), I became a sales manager and would travel across Madhya Pradesh in 38-degree heat. I was not entitled to an AC car. The reasoning was that if the company salespeople were expected to make forty sales calls in searing heat, it would be most unbecoming for the manager to look cool and well-turned-out when he or she entered the market.

Middle-class living can be a bit stifling too. HUL employees don't wear suits and ties but neither do they wear jeans and T-shirts. Just an ordinary shirt and trousers. It is neither the Silicon Valley culture nor is it the investment banking culture. The joke in office was that only the drivers and directors wore a tie and nowadays it is only the former who do.

One thing that has changed with time is the 'carpet and tea' rule. If you rose to become a work level (WL)-2C grade manager, you were entitled to a carpet in your room and a bearer who served you tea at designated times. With increasing space constraint, WL-2C managers started sharing office rooms with the more junior 2B. No matter. The carpets in the room were cut into half, notionally dividing the room, and the bearer would ignore the WL-2B manager and serve only the WL-2C manager in the room.

We have certainly inherited the idiosyncrasies of the rule- and status-conscious Indian middle class. But remember that means we have also inherited the best features of the Indian middle class: a hunger to grow and an inborn conservatism in costs.

Meritocracy

Meritocracy is a quintessential middle-class value. By dint of hard work and ability, you rise. Elite companies tend to become Old Boys' Clubs, while organizations that practise affirmative action sacrifice performance for a more representative employee base. At HUL, the culture of meritocracy is aided by clear goals, a system that rates performance and promotions that are dependent on a track record of performance.

Sanjay Dube, a former sales director at HUL, says that HUL's meritocracy is deeply nurturing, believing as it does that 'even the tallest trees were saplings once and needed nurturing'. He is against the cut-throat meritocracy of American companies and of investment banks, where you are only as good as the last deal or the last quarter's performance.

HUL's meritocracy is much more supportive. It identifies, picks and builds a leadership pipeline based on performance and persists with these leaders when they face difficult circumstances. Adversity is seen as a strong learning experience, especially early in careers. This builds leaders at the top who have seen rough times and hence navigate their teams through crises with much more maturity than what would be the case in a hard meritocratic system.

In 2009 when Nitin Paranjpe, currently COO of Unilever, was CEO of HUL, the company recorded one of its worst-ever years. Unilever declared a small bonus for the South Asia region overall, but Nitin felt that since the other countries in the region – Pakistan, Bangladesh and Sri Lanka – had done well it was only fair that India forgo its bonus entirely so that the others got a substantial amount. He gingerly raised the idea of a zero bonus with the management committee. He recalls how one director later told him he was offended that Nitin had even thought he had to ask such a question. Poor performance, the director said, merits no bonus and it would be a shame if the company accepted any bonus in a year like this.

Nitin himself, unlike the rest of HUL, was part of a larger Unilever bonus pool. Since Unilever had done well that year he was entitled to a bonus. But his conscience didn't allow him to take a bonus when his team got none. He wrote to his bosses in Unilever saying that he would like to forgo the bonus. After a few days of radio silence, his boss got back to him saying that while he appreciated the gesture, Nitin would have to accept the bonus since the principle of bonus works both ways. There could be years in which his team would earn a big bonus and he may not.

Admittedly, the system of meritocracy is far from perfect. HUL sometimes gets it wrong on promotions. But it gets it right more often than not for two reasons.

First, the HR department in HUL has more teeth than in other organizations. They will raise a red flag if a candidate has a poor performance record and will usually insist on formal interviews with the line manager and others on the interview panel.

Second, HUL has a much berated, non-official, batch system that prevents obviously biased promotions. You must have completed a certain number of working years before being considered for the next work level. For instance, you must be of the 2010 batch of MBAs before being considered for a WL-3 job in 2019. This government-inspired 'batch' system holds true for the first ten to twelve years of a person's career. After this, merit matters a lot more. Whether regressive or conservative, this system broadly works. This middle-class aspect of HUL prevents the anointment of early superstars, allows for late bloomers and checks wanton promotions.

Comfortable in Lakhimpur and in London

The third aspect of the HUL way that Harish stressed was a culture that can, as Rudyard Kipling put it, 'walk with Kings – nor lose the common touch'. R. Gopalakrishnan, former vice chairman of HUL and director in Tata Sons, says that to build an antenna one first needs to get the earthing done.

In 1979, when HUL faced a problem of poor milk yields in the catchment of its ghee and milk powder factory in Etah, Uttar Pradesh (UP), then chairman T. Thomas started sending management trainees to stay for eight weeks in a village in Etah district. They were to instil confidence among villagers to adopt artificial insemination of cows to improve the milk yield.

In January 2000, just after I joined HUL, my batchmate Shobhit and I were sent for our Etah stint. Our hosts were a poor farming family in Bakrai village close to the tehsil headquarter Patiyali, the birthplace of the thirteenth-century poet Amir Khusrau.

My target was to build a road in the village and to inseminate seventy-eight cows. We slept on a charpai inside a mud hut, performed our morning ablutions in the field outside, had a quick meal of potatoes and roti at 8 a.m. and then got on to a bike containing cryogenic cans with sperms.

Cows and milk are central to the agrarian economy of UP. To improve the milk yield of cows, the government was subsidizing the artificial insemination of cows with sperm from higher yielding varieties. HUL was supporting the cause. We roamed around villages trying to identify cows in heat. When we saw cows emitting a characteristic white discharge, we would meet the farmer and convince him of the merits of paying us Rs 10 to artificially inseminate his cow. Milk yield, we would argue, would go up from 4 litres to 10 litres if we crossed the Indian cow with a Jersey bull. After observing my boss Gautam do this a couple of times, I had a go at artificial insemination. Once I got over the squeamishness, it wasn't a very tough task. I can honestly say when asked in truth-or-dare sessions that I lost my virginity to a cow.

After a hard day's work, we would go back to our village. The Ganga was only a few kilometres away and occasionally we would saunter along its bank, take a quick dip in the icy-cold water and then smoke a chillum with the sadhus on the bank to warm ourselves. On most days we would simply get back to our adopted home, have yet another meal of roti and potato, warm ourselves by a fire and shut our eyes shortly after dusk.

While the first few days felt alien, we adjusted quickly and started enjoying our rural life. Maybe it is nostalgia, but I don't remember being healthier and happier than I was during our time there. I have made many visits to rural India since. But even now, when I think about how some product will work in rural India, my mind goes back to our time in the village in Etah.

Mohit Sud, currently the branch manager of HUL's Central India Branch, wrote a blog about his travails while travelling in buses in Tamil Nadu as a management trainee in 2004. These include words of wisdom such as 'Every

TN bus has overhead shelves all along the side of the bus to keep luggage. Unfortunately, the designer did not take into consideration the abysmal condition of roads in TN and that certain people such as me are above average height. Consequently, when the rubber and pothole meet, so will your head and the shelf' and 'If the seat in front of you is occupied by women then it is best to move back 2 seats. The primary reason for this word of caution is that on a long-distance journey the odds that the woman in front of you will throw up are 3:4.'

Swarnim Bharadwaj, global brand director on Lux, recalls how a graduate from the Faculty of Management Studies, Delhi, famously said in his recruitment interview that the smallest city he had been to in India was . . . Noida! He was selected but promptly dispatched to train in Bihar.

The Delhi boy reported in at the East branch office in Calcutta and the first thing he asked was where the nearest jewellery store was. When they asked why, the Delhi boy's answer had the whole office in splits. He had been told by friends and family that eligible bachelors like him were often kidnapped in Bihar and forcibly married, so he wanted to wear a ring and asked Swarnim to spread the word that he was well and truly married. While his stint had many memorable experiences, the joy of a rural wedding wasn't going to be one of them.

Dinesh Biddappa, a former HR director at HUL, recalls how when he was the HR manager in the Orai factory in UP, freshly minted management trainees had to go through the grind. The factory had just been set up. The temperature was 45 degrees-plus, the guest house was a ramshackle shed and food was insipid. But so used to hardships were the trainees that when he asked his HR trainee Piyush Mehta for suggestions to improve living conditions, Piyush merely said that everything was excellent, just that at night rats would come and nibble his ear. Was there any solution to this minor inconvenience?

If my own career in HUL started with a deep introduction to the real India, my taste for the high life came four years later, when I was a brand manager on Surf detergent. My boss Sanjay Behl, currently CEO of Raymond, asked me to accompany our director, Aart Weijburg, on a trip to Singapore. Aart was travelling to meet his boss for an annual presentation and wanted help with his presentation – or a 'bag carrier', as we brand managers called it.

I was given a wardrobe allowance of Rs 8000 to spruce up and travelled business class for the first time. I could sleep on a flat bed in the plane, watch a film of my choice and order cuisine I wanted rather than stomach the food wrapped in silver foil that was placed in front of me. When we got to Singapore, I stayed in a hotel on Orchard

Road that cost $250 a night, and Aart took me to a plush restaurant for dinner, where rice cost roughly my monthly salary. Coming from a middle-class background – with a teacher mother and engineer father – this was as alien to me as Etah had been. But it was all part of training in the CEO factory.

The Entrepreneur Professional

Although well paid, managers at HUL don't make the kind of money that entrepreneurs make. Yet HUL managers have consistently displayed an entrepreneurial zeal and owner's mindset that is the envy of most companies.

Gopal Vittal, a former director of HUL's Home Care and Personal Care and currently CEO of Bharti Airtel, says the entrepreneur professional mindset of HUL managers is a distinctive feature of the company. It is best exemplified by the fact that despite being a multinational, HUL has always been an insider in India.

In the early 1990s excise duties on personal products and cosmetics came down from 120 per cent to 50 per cent and then 30 per cent. HUL, through industry associations, had persuaded the government to do this, pointing out that the move would increase consumption and with it total tax collection. To successfully argue in favour of consumption, when it was a word treated with suspicion in the government, speaks of the high regard given to HUL. No multinational in India, Vittal says, could have manoeuvred such a move.

S. Ravindranath, a former director of Foods and Refreshments, talks about the time that Unilever decided to exit coffee globally and the India division was given a closure notice. The decision was based on an unarguable business rationale – the business was too small and capital-intensive and Nestlé was too formidable a competitor. However, the Bru team in India was unwilling to give up. They asked for a year to prove that they could create a profitable model. They created manufacturing capacity with minimal capital expenditure by challenging the output of the existing plant. They changed the advertising agency and relaunched the brand. As a result, the business was able to grow much faster at a much lower cost. Today Bru is one of HUL's most successful brands.

Examples of entrepreneurial professionalism do not extend only to big projects like excise duty reduction or shutting businesses. Nikhil Jacob, currently the general manager for coffee, recalls how HUL had planned to run a promotion on its products with the chips brand Lays in Bihar. The promotion was part of a shopping festival that many modern retailers run called 'Big Day' and was extremely time-sensitive. A delay would mean a loss in market share during these high peak days. Despite assurances there was a slip in logistics and the team had almost given up on the offer.

The sales manager of Bihar then messaged the team that she was going to buy Lays packets from the market to ensure that the promotion ran on time. The only problem was that in the middle of the night the only shops open were canteens in railway stations. No matter. The entire Bihar team was mobilized to wake up, go to the railway station closest to them, pick up as many packets of Lays as possible and come to Patna by 9 a.m. Some travelled as many as eight hours to get there on time. The promotion went off smoothly until the actual stocks of Lays arrived.

Not just HUL alumni, HUL kids too become CEOs very often. Rohit Ohri, CEO of the advertising agency FCBUlka, shares a story about his father, Gotam Ohri, a chemical engineer who worked in the Calcutta HUL factory as a department head, which illustrates the sense of ownership that company employees have. Once there was a surprise visit to the factory by the chairman T. Thomas. Ohri Sr, who was obsessed with factory floor cleanliness, asked a newly minted management trainee from a premier MBA institute to join the operations to clean the floor. Sensing his hesitation, Ohri Sr picked up a mop and started cleaning the floor himself. The message was clear to all: the factory was their karmabhoomi and all jobs were equally important here.

It is not easy to understand why a large company like HUL exhibits this kind of entrepreneurship. It is not a typical middle-class trait to believe that setbacks will happen, defeat will not. Most likely the early Indianization of the management from the 1950s resulted in a strong culture of ownership and institutional self-confidence. Then, as Sanjay Dube says, since 'most leaders are high achievers in their academic career, they bring a confidence that is reinforced by the institutional self-confidence they encounter'. Culture reinforces culture.

Unchanging Value System

The final ingredient is old-fashioned goodness. Rohit Kale, CEO of the storied headhunting firm Spencer Stuart, told me that they only use HUL products in his house. His father had passed away while still a young manager at HUL. The company gave his mother a job and paid every rupee of his education until the day he got his first job.

It is not only care for one's own. As thanksgiving for the removal of price control in the 1970s, T. Thomas handed over a prime piece of real estate in South Mumbai to Mother Teresa's Missionaries of Charity. Asha Daan continues as a home for destitute to this day, paid for by HUL.

But the one value of HUL that stands out is its

unbending integrity. In 1997 Nitin Paranjpe was promoted to branch manager of the Madras branch, HUL's largest region. He had been a highly successful brand manager on Vim, launching the famous Vim Bar, and was given a job usually reserved for much more senior managers. Shortly after he took over, retailers in Kerala started agitating for higher margins from consumer goods companies. Thinking that if the largest company caved in, the rest would follow, the retailers announced a boycott of HUL products.

Nitin recalls how Keki Dadiseth, then chairman, called him and said, 'Nitin, I'm not calling to put you under any pressure but to let you know that you are the man on the ground. No one will double-guess you and you will call the shots. You take any decision and we will back you to the hilt.' Despite having almost no sales for several months, Nitin and HUL stuck to their guns. Nitin says, 'It's easy to talk values when there is nothing at stake, but sticking to it when the business is under deep decline due to a state not functioning is unique to HUL.'

During my sales training as a management trainee I was posted in Surat. Sundays were off but I wasn't expected to leave the town. My home town of Mumbai being only four hours away, I decamped for the day but signed myself present on the roster. While it was far from my intention, the consequence of this was that I was given a daily allowance of Rs 50 for staying in Surat for the day that I was in Mumbai. I was found out by my boss Shailendra Gupte. This was a major misdemeanour in HUL books, and I should have been sacked on the spot. But after a long cathartic session, he did something unprecedented: he let me off. I am out of touch with Shailendra, but I want him to know that if I were a religious person, he would be in my prayers every day.

The HUL principle of integrity extends from small matters to big issues. After the goods and services tax (GST) was implemented in the middle of 2017, followed by the rate changes in December 2017, the government asked companies to pass on the benefits to consumers but did not lay down the rules detailing how the benefit should be passed. This was complex, as taxes had gone up on some products and gone down on others. For example, how does one pass on a 7 per cent tax saving on a Re 1 shampoo sachet? Our current chairman, Sanjiv Mehta, decided to unilaterally pass the net benefits of GST in total to consumers. But there was the pipeline to be taken care of – stocks already produced, packed and shipped to the depots. How was one to reduce prices on it?

HUL took the unprecedented step of calculating all benefits that simply could not be passed on to consumers and voluntarily offered to pay the government the amount. The government was stumped. Never had someone volunteered to pay money back. There was simply no mechanism to take back the money, except through a fine. It took the government many months to accept the money offered by HUL. The government went through several rounds of discussions and finally levied on us an amount in excess of what we had offered. Similarly, they then raised claims on several other FMCG companies. HUL contested the claim and obtained a stay on the demand for part of the payment. The matter is sub judice. Many people in the industry remind us that none of this would have happened if HUL had not voluntarily decided to pay the money to the government in the first place. Yet all of us steeped in HUL culture know that we would rather pay it upfront and without a prompt than pay in reputation.

And then there are the smaller matters. Once my colleague Sandeep Kohli's bag got exchanged with another person's at the airport. When he reached home, he found that the bag contained a stash of cash. The owner's name and number were in the bag too. He promptly called the owner, who sounded quite relaxed. He had seen Sandeep's visiting card in the bag. Since his bag had obviously been mixed up with someone from HUL, he knew he had nothing to worry about. His money would go nowhere.

In India, companies often end up in situations that require greasing of palms. Many companies choose the expedient route. But a culture of winking at graft doesn't just extend to the outside world. It gradually eats the insides of the company like a cancer. HUL, like the Tatas, has thrived for so long due to this one non-negotiable value – integrity. We don't pay bribes. Full stop.

In this chapter, we looked at the middle-class value system that is the DNA of HUL. These are the five attributes Indian industry loves in HUL CEOs. The next chapter talks about the discipline that HUL and its CEOs are most famous for: marketing.

Summary

1. If one were to name an Indian company that has been successful for over a hundred years and continues to be wildly successful it would be HUL.
2. Many achievements: what stands out is being a school for Indian CEOs – **A CEO Factory**.
3. Five ingredients that define the company that we can emulate in our professional lives:
    *   **A middle-class soul** – aspiring to grow, conservative on costs.
    *   **A meritocratic culture** – only people with a track record of performance promoted.
    *   **Walk with kings and yet have the common touch**

– managers at home in the remotest villages while also speaking to investment bankers in South Mumbai.

- **Entrepreneurial professionals** – will go the extra mile to deliver results.
- **Unbending integrity** – the company would rather close operations than compromise on values.

4. Paradoxically, to succeed in India in the long term you have to stay honest.

2

Why Marketing Is Business

Marketing Lessons from Hindustan Unilever

'We are essentially a marketing company . . . Marketing to us is a total operation, more than mere selling. It has a wide band of activity, from product development to consumer satisfaction.' P.L. Tandon, HUL's first Indian chairman, 1960

Marketing = What the Consumer Wants

'What is marketing, uncle?' asked a friend's twelve-year-old son the other day. I was unable to give a straight answer. In most companies – and indeed in the layperson's understanding of the word – marketing is tom-tomming the product or service that the company offers. In short it is the publicity department. It has a negative connotation and is often used as a back-handed compliment. When people say 'ABC politician is a marketing genius' they imply that he doesn't really have content but through clever talk has convinced people to vote for him. In HUL that is what we would call advertising.

For HUL marketing is the nodal function that sits at the heart of the business. It frames business problems in consumer terms, understands unmet consumer needs and then mobilizes the rest of the company into fulfilling it. You could also call marketing at HUL the Department of Meeting Consumer Needs, which is what the whole company is supposed to be doing. **In HUL marketing is *the* business.**

In technology companies what HUL calls marketing is a combination of the product department and the marketing department. From a tech company point of view, understanding what the 'customer'* wants, developing a cool product and letting people know about it come under the purview of marketing.

At HUL the brand team is usually at the centre of fundamental business problems such as cost structures, capacity utilization and technology. Nitish Bhalotia, currently general manager laundry, writes about how as brand manager on Surf Excel he was central to solving a key business issue faced by Surf Excel – that of value and affordability. Surf Excel was a strong brand, but unaffordable. Surf Excel Blue, the good old Surf, was affordable but its blue colour and fluffy texture were considered old-fashioned. The one competitive advantage of Surf Excel Blue was that it was made with a technology called spray-drying, which was difficult to replicate. By challenging dominant logic and making a virtue of its fluffiness (it dissolves better) and its blue colour

---

* What tech companies call customer, HUL calls consumer; customers for HUL are the shopkeepers who sell to consumers.

(connoting clean) the team was able to exponentially grow the spray-drying segment of the market. Great marketing moved consumer preference to a part of business that HUL had a fundamental competitive advantage in.

What Is a Brand?

'What is a brand?' is as tricky a question as 'What is marketing?' I like to think of brands as *trust-marks that have a few specific associations for many consumers.* Marking A on a bag of wheat is a mark, but it is a trust-mark when many people trust that A on a bag of wheat means that it is good quality wheat.

A trust-mark signifying quality is a necessary but not sufficient condition for a good brand. A good brand also has a few other specific associations for many. The sharper the associations and the more people who know the association, the stronger the brand.

Ask consumers to close their eyes and say what comes to mind about the brand Lifebuoy. Chances are they will say, 'Soap. Red. Germkill. Rectangular. Doctor. Strong smelling.' Ask them to think about brand Horlicks and they will say, 'Powder. White. Milk. Nutritious. Mum gave it to me as a child.' Think of your favourite brands and repeat the exercise. You will be able to form very sharp associations that several people share.

Consumers use brands as a shorthand to navigate an increasingly complex world. The other day my wife and I were having an argument on which movie to see. My wife won the day by saying that the film she wanted to see was produced by Viacom 18. It would at minimum have a good story, be plausible and have character actors. Those are the brand associations that my former colleagues at HUL who run Viacom, Sudhanshu Vats and Ajith Andhare, have built over the last ten years.

Srirup Mitra, vice president of the soaps business, talks about how as a brand manager he built the Lifebuoy liquid handwash brand. While the main competitor was using claims around effectiveness, Srirup realized that washing hands with soap was a chore for kids before diving into their favourite food. This gave rise to an entirely new axis of superiority in this category – speed. The product was redesigned to deliver complete protection in ten seconds, and competitors were repositioned as 'slow and hence ineffective'. This was presented to consumers with one of the most memorable lines in recent soap advertising: *'Bunty, tera sabun slow hai kya?'* or 'Bunty is your soap slow?'

Other things being equal, consumers pay a significant premium for the simplicity in navigation that a good brand can bring. And unlike product quality or good pricing or easy availability (all of which require capital), building brands mainly requires intellectual capital. It is easily the best return on investment in most businesses.

At HUL marketing is a function that understands and solves consumer needs using brands.

Defining the Problem

My alma mater IIMA and HUL have had a very close relationship over the years. Some of HUL's best marketeers, Vindi Banga, Hemant Bakshi, Mukul Deoras and Sudhanshu Vats, have come from IIMA. HUL has played a key role in the development of IIMA. Every single HUL chairman has been a guest of honour at IIMA's annual convocation and the first Indian chairman of HUL, P.L. Tandon, was one of its founders.

One of the most iconic marketing professors at IIMA, Labdhi Bhandari, who is credited with playing a key role in developing marketing at the institute, was an HUL alumnus. The HUL way of marketing and the IIMA way of marketing have had a symbiotic relationship. Nowhere is this more apparent than in problem-framing.

'What is the *problhem*?' Professor A.K. Jain would repeatedly ask us in a strong voice, a slight nasal emphasis on the operative word.

Bearing a striking resemblance, both physical and otherwise, to Robin Williams in the film *Good Will*

Hunting, Professor Jain was one of those legendary IIMA professors. He joined the institute in 1969 and inspired scores of WIMWIans (WIMWI or Well-Known Institute of Management in Western India is how IIMA refers to itself in case studies written by its faculty) to join the marketing profession.

His 'Marketing 1' classes were an anomaly at IIMA in terms of the students' attention span. They would wash their face, look as presentable as they could and troop in a few minutes before time into the class. They remained alert through the class, if only to look away, deflect and hide when Professor Jain asked what he believed was the most fundamental question in marketing: 'What is the problem?'

I got the raw end of the deal in the first class. We had been given, as many batches before us, the case study of 'Nirdosh'. Nirdosh was a brand of herbal, zero-nicotine cigarettes. The problem before us was to segment potential consumers for these herbal cigarettes. Who would be the ideal customers for Nirdosh?

Our group feverishly burnt the midnight oil and came up with the idea of marketing Nirdosh to pregnant women, who were barred from nicotine. Full of excitement, we worked our way through the marketing plan.

The next morning, confident of the brilliance of our output, I volunteered to enlighten the class. Professor Jain listened with keen interest. A deafeningly silent pause later, he started out by complimenting the lateral thinking of our team. It was rare, and I think he meant it. He then went on to tell us a story about Mullah Nasreddin, the Central Asian wit.

A friend saw Mullah Nasreddin searching frantically for his key under a street lamp. The friend joined him and a few minutes later when neither met with any success he asked Nasreddin whether he was sure he had dropped the key right there. Nasreddin said no, he had dropped it in a darker corner of the street but was looking for it here because there was more light here. Stinging point made, Professor Jain moved on to the next group.

I had been slapped. But he was right. Like Mullah Nasreddin, we too had found a problem to fit a brilliant solution, not a solution to the problem. We had been asked to segment the market for herbal cigarettes. Had we done a thorough enumeration of all segments? Apart from pregnant women, those wanting to give up cigarettes, nature lovers, party smokers could all have been valid segments. Had we assessed the potential size of each segment? Or had we decided to target a segment based on ability to win in that segment or just because we thought it was a cool segment to target?

Just a few years ago I developed a small tabletop ice cream freezer. I convinced the organization that this was the ideal solution to make ice cream available in very small shops in cities like Mumbai. Unfortunately, while the size of the freezer was a fifth that of a normal ice cream cabinet, it consumed three-fourths the electricity. Though we had solved the space issue, the revenue per cabinet did not justify the cost of electricity. Another case of a solution finding a problem. I had not learnt my lesson from Professor Jain well enough.

Class after class, Professor Jain would spend inordinate time defining the problem. Was loss of market share the problem for a brand or was it just symptomatic of a deeper problem of falling brand equity? Was brand equity the real problem or was it again symptomatic of poor advertising? Sometimes it felt tedious, but Professor Jain's belief was drill the problem deep enough and the solution emerges.

Marketing as a discipline started growing on me, just as did the architecture of our campus. Built by the modernist Louis Kahn, the red-brick structures of IIMA are studied by architecture students all over the world. I used to wonder why at first. The bricks had faded, there were deep cracks visible and the walls would feel moist in the monsoon.

But intoxication takes time. The graceful arches, the monastic dorms and the beautiful, ever-changing interplay of sunlight and shadows gave me several hours of pleasure. I would sit at the Louis Kahn Plaza and focus on the symmetry of the several windowless openings of the faculty section. I would then close my eyes and open them gradually. An entirely different perspective would emerge, and the building would transcend into something monumental, as if something had emerged by itself from the landscape.

Professor Jain once told us to look at problems in a similar manner. Alternate time between the narrow gaze of depth, facts, data and analysis with the broad gaze of synthesis, open-ended thoughts and imagination. Take the worm's view, then take the bird's view.

If Professor Jain taught the doyens of HUL problem-framing, then the famous WAC course taught us problem-structuring.

Shortly before I joined IIMA, Vish Uncle, an alumnus from the 1971 batch, gave me a REM or a remedial session. He told me that the only thing that stayed with him thirty years after leaving IIMA was the WAC class. Take it seriously, he said.

WAC, short for written analysis and communication, was meant to improve our writing and communication skills. We were given a case and within a strict word limit had to write a solution to it. Since I was an English-speaking type who had won creative writing contests in college festivals, I thought I would ace this course. My essay was laced with graceful phrases and wit and quotations from famous people. I was confident of getting an A. I landed a C–, probably the lowest grade in the batch.

Sendil, my dorm senior and a doctoral student, took me under his wing. WAC was not a course in literature, he told me. It was a course in structuring a solution to a problem. The recommended WAC structure was dogma. You first had to synthesize the case into a paragraph called the 'situation analysis'. This was not a summary of the case but a set of inferences from the case that help in identifying the problem at hand.

Imagine the scene in *Dilwale Dulhaniya Le Jayenge*, where Raj meets Simran in the mustard field of Punjab and sings 'Tujhe Dekha'. The situation analysis would be:

Raj, spoilt, wealthy NRI, with hidden Indian values, has followed his beloved Simran to India. Simran is due to get married to big Jat man (BJM) in 30 days.

Once you had analysed the situation, you had to state, in a crisp sentence, the decision that the protagonist of the case had to take. This was the same as Professor Jain's problem definition. In this instance: *'How should Raj ensure that Simran marries him and not BJM?'*

Once the decision to be taken was stated, we had to enumerate all the possible options. The options, as our statistics professor Madhavan would say, had to be mutually exclusive and collectively exhaustive. The options here include *elope with Simran, reveal himself and ask Simran's father for her hand, without revealing himself prove to Simran's family that he is a better catch than the BJM or kill BJM.*

Once the options had been enumerated we had to, in order of priority, list the criteria that we would use to select the best option. In this case in order of priority they would be *follow the law, get blessings of parents, maximize probability of getting the girl.*

In the final evaluation of options it doesn't take much to figure that Raj will have to surreptitiously try to get Simran's parents to like him over thirty days and live with the risk of getting beaten by BJM. As Sherlock Holmes said in 'The Sign of the Four', 'when you have eliminated the impossible, whatever remains, however improbable, must be the truth'.

Holmes might even have managed a B+ in WAC. Shah Rukh Khan would have got an A−.

Problem structuring and written communication are fundamental traits required not just in marketing but in general management. Find the nearest CEO you know or if you don't know one look up a TED Talk of a CEO you admire. Beneath the spit and polish will be super sharp problem definition and very simple communication.

There is of course much more to marketing than problem definition and structuring. It was appropriate that the very last class I attended at IIMA was a guest lecture by former HUL chairman Dr Ashok Ganguly. Ramrod straight and dignity personified, Dr Ganguly was a legend not just in HUL but in corporate India. He was a Padma Vibhushan, a Rajya Sabha member and the winner of multiple lifetime achievement awards. He spoke from the heart, with a sprinkling of wit.

He recounted how once in the 1980s, a cabinet secretary asked him patronizingly, 'Well, Mr Ganguly, still selling soap?' Without missing a beat Mr Ganguly replied, 'Well Mr Cabinet Secretary, still having a bath?' Dr Ganguly's class had a simple message to marketeers. The essential ingredient to succeed in marketing in particular, and life in general, is to move out of one's comfort zone, from problems using Microsoft Excel in air-conditioned office rooms into the heat, grime and dust of rural India. Depth of experience, not problem-solving ability alone, was the heart of marketing.

The 'Job to Be Done'

The job to be done (JTBD) process is the HUL way of framing and structuring problems.

HUL's annual marketing calendar starts around June with the framing of JTBD for the coming year. This is often a routine process with JTBD of the previous year carried forward. Occasionally, a brilliant new JTBD that gives fresh impetus to a business is created. Unilever defines a JTBD as 'get who to do what'. A JTBD could be 'get middle-aged, middle-income women in small towns to start drinking green tea' or 'get rural users of Clinic Plus shampoo to use it a bit more often'.

Framing a JTBD is subtler than it sounds. It involves making a series of difficult choices. But to make choices, as we saw in the IIMA WAC processes, one must first lay down the alternatives. The 'Get Who' is the more complex question but at its simplest you can talk to non-users, light users or heavy users of either your brand or the category by getting them to do one of three things – increase the number of users (called 'penetration' in the jargon), increase the frequency of usage or increase the consumption per use.

The mathematically inclined among us will immediately see that at its simplest there are nine JTBDs that are possible: three types of users of either the brand or category into doing one of three things. From getting non-users of the hair conditioner category to adopt it to getting light users of Sunsilk conditioners to use it once more to getting heavy users of Sunsilk to use two handfuls on the hair.

Selecting the JTBD needs criteria. The simplest criterion that I have seen while taking business decisions is a 2x2 matrix plotting *size of prize* (how many fruits on the tree) on one axis and *ease of winning* (how easy is it to climb the tree) on the other axis. The ideal choice is of course to do something with high impact of size of prize and high probability of success or ease of winning. In other words, find the tree with the most fruits that is also the easiest to climb.

Take any decision you want to make and plot it on such an axis. I have been trying to lose weight unsuccessfully for the past several years. Now I have decided to give it another shot. There are four possible ways (see Figure 3.1). Stopping carbs is a sure shot way, but it is hard. Cutting fats is an equally hard way, but my dietician friend tells me I will eat more carbs and cutting fats will actually make

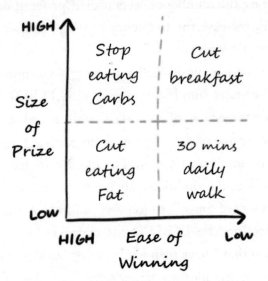

Figure 3.1: Choosing Weight-Loss Strategies

no difference. Walking for 30 minutes a day is easy, but unlikely to make a difference. So I have decided to cut breakfast. Looking at results and my mood at 12 noon though, I might have to opt for the fourth quadrant.

For each JTBD, size of prize must be thought out on a case-by-case basis but there are some general rules of thumb for ease of winning. Counter-intuitively, **it is easier to grow a category than it is to grow a brand.** This is because an under-penetrated category represents an unsolved consumer problem (assuming the category solves a problem in the first place!) while growing brand penetration in an already penetrated category means nudging out a competitor who has more or less solved the problem. Of course, one should attempt to grow a category only if one is the market leader; otherwise the fruits of your labour will land in the lap of a competitor. I recall an example of how Unilever patiently developed the market for single-use detergent tablets in the UK, only to hand over the category to a bigger competitor who entered later.

Similarly, **it is much better to target non-users and light users, because heavy users of a category or brand know it so well that they are difficult to influence any further. Finally, increasing number of users is much easier than increasing frequency of usage.** And it is almost impossible to influence consumption per use. The only apocryphal case that I have heard of is a toothpaste manufacturer who increased paste per brush by increasing the diameter of the nozzle! But in general, once people have bought a brand or category they titrate usage for themselves and while they can change it themselves it is hard for marketeers to influence this. For years Surf would give free buckets with its large 4 kilo pack hoping that consumption among users who used a little bit of Surf and lots of cheap powder would increase. But consumption didn't move at all and consumers only ended up buying Surf less frequently.

In summary it is easiest to get non-users of a category to adopt the category (get chai users to drink green tea) and it is the toughest to get heavy users of a brand to consume more of it (drink four cups of Brooke Bond Red Label every day rather than two). A lot of the evidence for this argument can be found in the brilliant book *How Brands Grow* by Byron Sharp. As a practitioner I have found Sharp's principles working for me time and again.

Implied here is one key factor about marketing: **at HUL marketing is not seen just as a 'wishy-washy' creative role. It is clearly defined and carefully planned, and the problem and market are properly quantified. It is a science as much as an art.** Anyone who takes marketing seriously and wants to see it enabled at scale will need to adopt this thinking.

I would be giving away confidential data if I wrote about some of our JTBDs for HUL's existing brands, but one that is in the public domain already is why HUL choose to acquire GlaxoSmithKline (GSK) India in 2018.

Buying Horlicks, the HUL way

When GSK India with its marquee brands Horlicks and Boost went up on the block, HUL was faced with the question of whether to bid for it or not. The brands had a glorious history but of late had not been performing very well. There was a concern that the category was past its prime.

It was clear to our CFO Srinivas Phatak and me that deciding to go for this major acquisition based on entering new categories would be speculative. We had to be sure that Horlicks and Boost had JTBD that had a large size of prize – and that they were relatively easy to do.

While assessing the category we realized that only 25 per cent of Indian households have a nutrition drink (HFD or health food drink) once a year or more. Even those who drink it regularly do so only once in three to five days. Despite this constraint, the category size was over Rs 7000 crore. So assuming that we could get the balance

75 per cent into the category and that consumption increased with time, there was enormous money to be made. A large size of prize.

The heartland of the HFD category in India is the South and the East. Many efforts to convert non-users in the North and the West have failed for a number of reasons. So to look to convert non-users in the North and the West would be speculative. But in the South and the East we realized that while urban markets were well penetrated, rural markets remained under-penetrated. To give an example: urban penetration of coffee and of HFD were similar but rural penetration of HFD was half that of coffee. The reasons for this were many but we had a large and relatively easy JTBD for our Horlicks acquisition: 'Get rural consumers in the South and East of India to try the HFD category'. Category focused, non-user focused and penetration focused.

Having defined both the problem and the solution in the HUL way, we decided to acquire GSK. We paid Rs 32,700 crore, in the largest deal in the FMCG sector that the country has seen.

Marketing: What Works, What Doesn't

In the following sections, I will look at HUL's learnings over the years.

Do segmenting and targeting work?

Segmentation (dividing the consumers into clusters), targeting and positioning are the fundamental pillars of marketing strategy taught at any B-school. It is the Philip Kotler way of marketing. Within this, segmentation is usually considered the heart of marketing and all marketing thought has to start from rigorous segmentation. After twenty years at HUL, I have a more nuanced view of segmenting and its relative importance.

For one, **in any category or for that matter in any behaviour, most human beings tend to want the same things and behave in a surprisingly similar manner.** For instance, a report during the heyday of the TV serial *Kyunki Saas Bhi Kabhi Bahu Thi* said that for every demographic – income, town, class and geography – the soap was number 1 in terms of ratings. Poornima from Peddar Road spent her leisure time the same way as Geeta from Gorakhpur.

Second, **when there are differences between segments, marketeers tend to take more decisive targeting options than required.** It is true that rich kids tend to watch more football and less cricket than kids from middle-class backgrounds. But such targeting misses two points. Despite watching less cricket than middle-class kids, rich kids watch a lot more cricket than football. Also, despite watching much less football than rich kids, the total time spent on football by middle-class kids is much more than by rich kids given the larger middle-class numbers. If you wanted to build football in India and targeted only more affluent youth, you would be missing out on middle-class kids at your peril.

An easy but often problematic way of segmenting India is by using states as a segmenting variable. But an inherent bias exists here. Political boundaries are man-made and arbitrary. Between states that are geographically far apart like Punjab and Tamil Nadu there are fundamental consumer differences, but between contiguous states there is little difference. At HUL this is best manifest in what we call 'the Kerala–Orissa problem'. Due to size and slightly lower income both these states are deemed less lucrative for most categories compared to their respective neighbours Tamil Nadu and West Bengal. As a result, despite being very similar to their larger cousins at an individual consumer level, many categories will have very high media investment in Tamil Nadu and West Bengal, but almost none in Kerala and Orissa. An incorrect segmentation, leading to forced targeting, leading to incorrect actions.

This is not to say that segmentation does not work. Just that it is better to start with broad segments and narrow it down only when there is compelling evidence. Harish

Manwani believes there are broadly only two benefits segments in personal care – beauty and health. Again, in foods there is taste and health. My former colleague P. Govind Rajan did a brilliant piece of work several years ago showing that attitudes and cultural acceptance of beauty varied dramatically across regions in India. He defined an index called 'beauty quotient' which was the highest in the North-East followed by West Bengal and lowest in the South. The higher the beauty quotient, the more the purchasing of this category. This showed that in some regions despite lower incomes (20 per cent lower) the propensity to buy beauty products was higher (25 per cent higher), Bengal being one example. So segmentation does work at a very simple, top level, but it is fair to say that we marketeers have a tendency to over-segment.

On the whole I can bet that most of us are targeting segments that are too narrow, based on biases that are not reflective of the people who are really consuming our category. The HUL way of segmentation is to stick to a fundamental, evidence-based segmentation – if at all.

Are you a Ferrari or a Nano?

If a brand is a set of associations that consumers have about a product, then positioning is guiding those associations to your advantage. A brand can be thought of as premium or mass (that is, value) due to a series of random marketing activities. But if the marketeer has a priori decided that she wants the brand to have a premium association and acts consistently in accordance with it, then it is good positioning.

While premium and mass are the most prominent positioning shorthand, give it enough thought and you realize they are problematic. Some people are willing and able to pay for a product with all the bells and whistles – a Ferrari, for example – while others are happy with a machine that takes them from place A to place B. But that doesn't mean they want to buy something that is positioned as mass. As Ratan Tata said, this was the mistake the Tatas made with the Nano. Positioning it as 'cheap' only meant that it was a social embarrassment to buy. Regardless of what they buy, consumers want products that are not positioned as value.

Before understanding how to position, it is important to understand why to position a brand. Plenty of evidence suggests that the biggest factor that drives purchase of brands in a category is 'salience'. If you are the most remembered brand in the category, chances are that you are also the most bought. Most of marketing is about being salient. But to be salient you need to have a few rich associations. This is where positioning comes in.

HUL uses a positioning technique called 'NeedScope'

which is based on the premise that human beings remember and identify best with personalities. Invented by Professor Heylens and originally called the Heylens map, the tool borrows from Jungian archetypes and the Freudian ego-id theory. The X-axis is an 'affiliative vs individualistic' axis – think of it as 'We vs I'. The Y-axis is an 'extrovert vs introvert' axis. In this context, the introvert doesn't mean someone who is quiet but someone who gets their energy from within. An extrovert is someone who gets their energy from outside.

NeedScope is complicated even for those who have spent a lot of time on it. Jung himself spoke of archetypes like mother, hero, magician and seductress that human beings across cultures quickly relate to. But the best explanation that I have heard of for NeedScope was from my senior colleague Sanjay Sachdeva.

He showed us clips from the Karan Johar classic *Kabhi Khushi Kabhie Gham*. Kajol as the belle from Chandni Chowk – warm, talkative, bubbly – was the archetype Extrovert-Affiliative sitting squarely at 2 o'clock on the NeedScope map (see Figure 3.2). Jaya Bachchan – loving, kind and a little repressed – was the classic mother archetype, Introvert-Affiliative at 4 o'clock on the map. Amitabh – stern, disciplined, self-centred and in control – was individualistic and introverted. He is 7 o'clock on the map. And Kareena as the unforgettable Poo – daring,

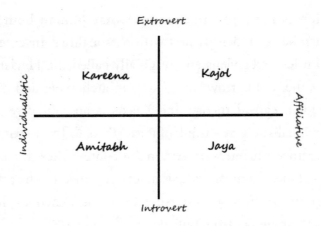

Figure 3.2: Sanjay's K3G Model of Positioning

flamboyant and vibrant – is a great example of 10 o'clock on the map.

In HUL we tend to speak of positioning in terms of times on this map. 'Kwality Wall's is a 2 o'clock brand but this poster looks so 7 o'clock' is a common refrain you will hear in marketing meetings. Most strong brands or people you know will be easy to position on a NeedScope map. Apple and McDonald's at 2 o'clock, Dove and Brooke Bond at 4 o'clock, Samsung and Domex at 7 o'clock and Lux and Thums Up at 10 o'clock. Think again of all the memorable people you know. They will be quite easy to place on the NeedScope map. The easier to place on the map, the better positioned they are, and the better positioned, the better remembered.

Since brand positions don't change often, all HUL categories and brands are mapped on the NeedScope map once every five years or so. Each brand has a desired place on the map and then there is an actual place. In the tea category our objective was to have Lipton at 2 o'clock, Brooke Bond at 4 o'clock, Taj at 7 o'clock and Taaza at 10 o'clock. The last exercise carried out several years ago indicated that Brooke Bond Red Label was in the centre of the NeedScope map: it meant everything to everybody. HUL has since spent years of patient work to move the brand on the map, and it is now a much sharper 4 o'clock.

Why Kissan Chilli Sauce didn't work, and other extension stories

Brand extensions are so ubiquitous that several people seem to think of them as a basic principle of marketing. If you have a brand that is strong and you are ambitious, then surely it makes sense to extend the brand into new categories. Even the most ambitious brand extension fanatics will agree that certain guardrails must be maintained – you can't extend a baby food brand into the condom category. But if you have these guardrails in mind, not extending the brand, the votaries of brand extensions argue, shows a lack of growth mindset.

The problem is brand extensions rarely work. As a management trainee I sold Kissan jam and ketchup in the market. Try as we did, 90 per cent of sales were Kissan Mixed Fruit Jam 500 grams and Tomato Ketchup 1 kilo. No one was really buying Kissan Chilli Sauce or Mango Jam. I saw this once again when I was the Foods and Refreshments director. Though Kissan had so many choices on offer, it was the same two packs that accounted for 90 per cent of Kissan sales. It was not for want of trying – we had entered staples, HFDs and even soy juices with the brand apart from umpteen variants of jams and sauces. Imagine if we had poured all that investment into the two products that actually sold in the market.

What was going on was actually very simple. If brands are a set of associations that consumers have, then it is very difficult to build new associations easily. Kissan is mixed fruit and tomato. There just isn't enough mind space for a new association. Even worse than building new unrelated associations is building associations that contradict the current one. In these cases the extension may unfortunately actually succeed but it is always at the expense of the main product. A case of operation successful but patient is dead.

Our former foods director Gunendar Kapoor once told us the story of Lux and Lux International. When Lux International was launched at a price higher than

Lux, Lux consumers felt that their good old Lux was no longer the best beauty soap on earth. At the same time Lux International consumers felt that they were paying a premium for ultimately what was just Lux. Before these contradictions could hurt the brand from either side, Lux International was replaced by Dove, a Unilever brand.

Rin on the other hand was not as lucky. Made famous by the iconic *'Bhala uski sari meri sari se safed kaise'*, Rin was the most popular detergent bar in the country. In the early 1990s HUL launched Rin Shakti – a cheaper version of the Rin brand. Rin Shakti volumes exploded, becoming bigger than Rin. To make the original Rin more attractive it was relaunched as Rin Supreme. But to no avail – why buy an expensive Rin when a cheaper Rin was available. After some time, Rin Shakti too slowed down. Was this the real Rin, consumers asked. Rin with its confused positioning was ripe for disruption. That is what almost happened.

It is to the credit of Unilever's current COO, Nitin Paranjpe, that HUL made an incredibly bold move. HUL renamed Rin Supreme as Surf Excel Bar and Rin Shakti became Rin. We would rib the project manager Rohit Bhasin on what we called 'Project Daulatabad' after the ill-fated move by Muhammad bin Tughlaq to move India's capital to Daulatabad. Half the consumers would perish during the migration, we would tease him, and the other half during the reverse migration. Luckily for HUL, we were proved wrong, and between Rin and Surf bars, HUL continues its lead in the detergent bars market.

As brand manager of Persil laundry powder in the UK, I came across another case of a deadly extension. Persil is one of the most famous brands in the UK. Posh Spice of the Spice Girls fame once said she wanted to be as famous as Persil. Built for fifty years on the single line 'Persil washes whiter', Persil had a 45 per cent market share of the UK market. In 1983 Persil added enzyme to its powder in order to remove stains better. Enzymes were an old technology in laundry powder and had been proven to be safe for many years. However, the mother of a three-year-old boy claimed that he had got eczema after wearing clothes washed in the new Persil. All hell broke loose in the British media and the story was headline news for several days. Instead of either sticking to its stand or withdrawing the new Persil entirely from the market, Unilever made on retrospect an error. It kept the new Persil, calling it Persil-Bio, but additionally brought back the old Persil, calling it Persil Non-Bio. It solved the problem temporarily, but in the longer term Persil Bio consumers were left wondering if it was safe enough and Non-Bio consumers whether it was efficacious enough.

Don't brand extensions work at all? In my years with HUL I have known only three where I can conclusively say that the extension grew the overall franchise. Dove shampoo, Surf Excel Matic and Red Label Natural Care. In all three cases the extensions did three things:

1. In no way did they implicate the performance of the 'core'. If you wash in a bucket, use Surf Excel, but if you have a machine, use the Matic version.
2. They solved real and meaningful consumer problems: Red Label Natural Care solves the need for many consumers to add spices to make tea tastier.
3. They all built from the fundamental associations of the brand: Dove soap was about care as was Dove shampoo.

Whether you are a brand manager launching an extension or a director of an MBA school launching a one-year variant of the school's flagship two-year programme, think long and hard. If you are lucky your extension will fail but if you are unlucky it may succeed and destroy the mother ship.

This principle is not applicable to the launch of brand extensions alone. Think of your own life and ask how much you want to extend yourself versus how much you want to do better in what you do well. If you play tennis well, should you try to improve your tennis or start playing badminton? If you are good at writing, should you aim to be the best writer in the world or start improving your mathematics? There is a tendency in all of us to do more rather than to do better. More rarely works.

Not everyone is Steve Jobs

Collecting quantitative consumer evidence before taking a marketing decision is close to a religion in HUL. For instance, if HUL were the publisher of this book they would first ask me to write a one-paragraph summary of the book. Then they would ask 300 consumers from at least two cities if they found it unique, relevant and credible and whether they would buy it. Readers, like consumers, tend to want to read more than they actually do, so HUL would then compare their scores on my book with scores on previous bestsellers. If it fared well, I would get my contract.

But wait, there is more. On my completing the book, HUL would repeat the same test but this time with a final book rather than a summary. If the scores compared to bestsellers were green, they would make the decision to publish. All publicity material will go through the same testing protocol and if the publisher wanted to change the second edition from a hardbound to a paperback, they would do another test and give both options to readers to choose from. If the publishing industry did this, the costs of the market research would exceed the revenue from the book. Sometimes this is the case in HUL too. We call it death by market research!

But I love market research. So much so that I got married to someone from the HUL market research department. We like to think that our kids are the perfect product of marketing and market research.

The best market research is, as Professor Jain taught, spending lots of time with a few well-chosen consumers. You can almost always get an answer to the question you want; though if you are not careful, you may even get the answer you want. This is one of the pitfalls of qualitative market research. Consumers tend to want to keep the interviewer happy and have a keen sense of what she wants to hear. The second pitfall: **what consumers say is different from what they think is different from what they do.** You need to be skilled to decode the difference between the three.

A few tips on consumer interactions. First, do it yourself. It is never too early or too late. As Vijay Raj, Unilever's market research guru, says, 'Just as the most comprehensive of CVs is not good enough to recruit a candidate without an interview, the best market research reports are no substitute to meeting the consumer yourself when taking a business decision.'

Don't be impatient – ask the question you want answered and then demand to know why. Indulge in a lot of small talk but not too much random small talk. If I wanted to assess whether a twenty-five-year-old corporate executive will read this book, I might start off by asking her where she studied, a little bit about her school, the smells and sounds of her school library, her library teacher, her favourite books as a child and then move to what she is reading now.

At a natural juncture in the conversation I would move to her working life, the challenges she faces as a professional, as a woman, who does she ask for help, does she read anything that would help professionally. At this point I may introduce the idea of this book but only in the context of other potential books. Never letting her know what I was really after, circling but never really pouncing. When I get a sense of whether she would be interested or not in this book, only then would I, with more than 75 per cent of the interview over, move on to more direct questions. A couple of other things: never read from a questionnaire or take detailed notes while speaking. Record if you can or just make a few short notes when you sense energy in the room. And finally always be on the watch out for some blazing insight (we will come to what an insight is in the next section).

P.L. Tandon recalls how in the late 1930s when HUL set up a market research department, a visiting specialist couldn't believe it when every woman said that her husband 'buys and chooses' household grocery products. He probed a bit deeper and a consumer suddenly said, 'He chooses, but I tell him what to choose!' It was apparent to HUL way back in 1937 that women call the shots in their business.

Quantitative research at HUL is a necessary evil. Evil because the same result can be got much cheaper and faster through good qualitative work. Necessary because you can't ensure sound qualitative work throughout and the costs of wrong decisions can be high. Not everyone is Steve Jobs, who famously said Apple did no market research. But a good rule is that the amount at risk should at least be 50x the cost of quantitative research.

Apart from qualitative and quantitative research, HUL uses syndicated research. This is research bought off the shelf and available to all competitors. HUL buys three of these: one to measure market shares and sales from the store, another that studies monthly changes in consumer behaviour with respect to relevant categories and the third which measures what consumers think of your brand. These are typically very expensive studies and most companies may not need them. But to prevent the drinking of your own Kool-Aid, it is important to get a generally accepted external validation of how your business is performing.

The insight: What makes HUL marketing different

My colleague Shiva Krishnamurthy, an Amitabh fanatic, once told me that all of *Sholay* can be captured in one line that Sanjeev Kumar says: *Loha hi lohe ko kaat sakta hai* (Only iron can cut iron). What a brilliant insight!

If there is one thing that differentiates Unilever marketing from the rest of the industry, it is in the use of insights. In fact, insights are the key not just to marketing problems but to business problems.

Definitions of insights are many. The one I remember is 'a penetrating understanding of your consumer that unlocks growth opportunities'. While useful, I find several issues with this definition. What does 'penetrating' mean, why only consumer and what if it does not unlock an opportunity? Does it cease to be an insight then? I prefer my own haiku: An insight is 'a contradiction that is obvious in hindsight' (think *Loha hi lohe ko kaat sakta hai*).

One of my early insights is one that I framed during my eight-week Etah stay. *'Dowry causes more births than deaths.'* The farmer I was staying with, Ramesh Chauhan, had two daughters and two sons. I gingerly asked him about family planning and was surprised to realize that he knew much more about it than I did. But the reason he had four kids was simple. Two boys were necessary – you need an heir and a spare. If he had had two boys, he would have stopped having more children. But every girl is a dowry out and needs to balanced by a dowry in – a boy. So when he had his first two girls, he knew he would be bankrupt unless he had two boys to balance the dowry. His gamble had paid off.

This insight, which by the way may not be statistically true, has all the building blocks required for insight framing. Find a link between disparate observations and express it pithily. Here there are two crucial pieces of data coming together, namely, population is a problem in India (especially in the rural UP) and Ramesh Chauhan had attributed his large family to the practice of dowry. I could simply have stated the insight as dowry is the cause of population growth in India. But a contradiction was missing. I used a third piece of data, 'dowry is synonymous with dowry deaths', to pithily frame what I think, even twenty years later, was a pretty good insight: *'Dowry causes more births than deaths.'*

One of my favourite insights is one that I saw several years ago on HUL's most controversial brand, Fair & Lovely. The insight was *'My gene pool is my destiny'*. I was dumbstruck. In six words the brand had captured the entire history of India, its cultural and political schisms and – without using the word – had put 'fair skin' at the heart of it. Another brilliant one was for the detergent brand Rin which was *'Unfair as it may seem, appearances can open and shut doors'*.

Another recent insight I framed was *'Those with money are thrifty, those without splurge'*. I was perplexed by a poor family I had met in Pune who had just splurged the previous night on a Magnum ice cream. The next family I met, much more middle class, never bought Magnum but bought the regular chocobar quite often. On the way back to Mumbai I was struck by the fact that the biggest market for Dove, HUL's premium soap, was rural Bihar, even though it was the poorest region of the country. Sappu, my Etah farmer's son, wore the same faded, frayed clothes every day and walked barefoot most of the time. But when he came into some money he went and bought himself an expensive pair of shoes. Middle-class people with a steady flow of income tend to optimize their spends across categories. The poor on the other hand operate in a more binary fashion – most of the time they make do without participating in a category, but on the rare occasion they do, they often buy the best.

Insights come in all sizes and shapes and are useful not just in marketing. An insight we had a few years ago on our ice cream model has transformed the business model for us. The insight *'To be viable enough to produce close to a big market, you have to first start producing close to the market'* was based on one observation: ice cream manufacturing which was capital-intensive was being done at a centralized location. This meant high distribution costs, high prices and low category consumption. Producing closer to the market allowed you to drop prices, which gave you an economic quantity that was enough to build the factory.

Framing insights requires three ingredients. The first is observation. You need to constantly read books, have conversations with interesting people and be consumer connected. The second is the ability to make lateral connections between disparate observations. This takes some conscious practise. And third, the ability to state the insight pithily.

But the benefits of insights are most dramatically visible when it comes to what a lot of people confuse with marketing: advertising. That is what we will see in the next chapter.

Before that, here is a summary of this chapter that builds the case that since marketing is business, every CEO should be a marketeer.

Summary

1. Marketing is at the heart of business. Great CEOs are great marketeers.
2. Marketing is neither advertising nor publicity. It understands consumer needs and solves consumer problems.
3. Brands are trust-marks with distinct associations for many consumers.

4. Building brands is a crucial competitive advantage for companies.

5. The marketing process starts by framing jobs to be done – get who to do what.

6. It is easier to get consumers to adopt a new category than to get them to increase consumption.

7. Broad segments are more representative of reality than a narrower segment.

8. Positioning is being clear on the brand associations you want to own.

9. Do not overextend your brand. Better to do what you do well rather than do new things.

10. The best market research is spending time personally with a few well-chosen consumers.

11. An insight is a 'contradiction that is obvious in hindsight'. Insight is the soul of marketing.

3

Be Famous Before Being Persuasive

Advertising and Media Lessons from Hindustan Unilever

Advertising is the sexiest part of marketing. And it is different from everything that comes before in this book and from what will follow. It is the only part of business management where both the right brain and the left brain, feeling and thought, magic and logic, are equally used. Though it can be learnt up to a point, very few people have a natural flair for it. While many people in advertising agencies have a natural flair, they often lack a strategic business perspective. If you have both, it is a serious competitive advantage.

While many of us may never make ads for television, all of us find the need to communicate simply. Some of us need to take the help of creative people to communicate better – a house we must build, a book cover we have to design or indeed a birthday party we have to organize. But getting the best out of creative people can be a tough task. The HUL approach to advertising is a great life skill to have.

HUL spends about Rs 3500 crore on advertising and accounts for roughly 15 per cent of spends and 20 per cent of the country's ads on TV (we buy much cheaper due to scale). Unilever believes that advertising is too important to be delegated. A senior person should lead the process from brief to production. That person can choose to consult with others or not. That's her call. But ultimately in advertising there should be one single decision maker, the advertising leader.

Be Clear on Who You Are

The most important thing in communication is not what you say, but whether you are true to who you are. Actions speak louder than words, as the cliché goes. So, **before you figure out what you want to say and how you want to say it, you have to be crystal clear on who you are.** In the case of brands, it goes back to positioning. Every piece of communication must reinforce the four or five associations consumers have about you. Why not keep building new associations with every piece of communication? The truth is that people have mind space only for a few key associations. Once built, it is difficult to add new ones and if you are not careful you will lose the old ones.

A few months ago, this picture (on the facing page) was going viral on the Internet. It is a composite of the

Courtesy of ZeeMelt/Kyoorius

top 44 Indian ads since the 1980s, all in a single painting. We can identify many of these ads partly because they were great and partly because they either leveraged or built memory structures that could be remembered in the absence of the brand name.

In the foreground is Zakir Hussain playing the tabla in a Taj Mahal tea ad. Over time Taj had moved away from using Zakir as its ambassador to use more conventional celebrities like Madhuri Dixit and Saif Ali Khan. In 2013, just as I was taking over the tea category marketing in HUL, I heard two youngsters saying Wah Taj when they spotted the santoor maestro Pandit Shivkumar Sharma at Mumbai airport. What a phenomenal memory structure to nurture.

We moved Taj back to its old memory structure – classical musicians (in three subsequent ads we have used Niladri Kumar, Rahul Sharma and Nirali Kartik as our ambassadors) playing mesmerizing music to the refrain of 'Wah Taj'. Taj advertising has suddenly become recognizable again and the brand has started gaining market share after a decade.

The iconic Flipkart campaign is of two kids who look like adults making e-commerce look like child's play. In 2015 I was asked to become a member of the Flipkart Advisory Board. Flipkart had recently changed the 'kids as adults' idea for their ad campaigns. I remember telling Mukesh Bansal (who ran the company at that time) and the newly appointed CMO, my former Lever colleague Samardeep Subandh, to revert to the old concept. It was a brilliant idea to show how simple e-commerce was (even kids could use it) and more importantly it was the brand's DNA. Samar, being an old Lever hand, thought the same way and the campaign went back to the earlier one.

Harish Manwani recalls how HUL's marketing guru Shunu Sen was in a meeting where managers were saying that everyone was using film stars and perhaps Lux should move on. Shunu said something on positioning that Harish hasn't forgotten: 'Anyone can use a film star but only Lux can carry it off.'

Brands become great because at some time in their past, even near past as the Flipkart example shows, someone has an epiphany or a lucky breakthrough. It is wise to distil this moment in a bottle and constantly take swigs from it. Brands that haven't had this epiphany need to understand their role in their consumers' life and constantly look for clarity and insight. The moment will come, sometimes sooner and sometimes later, but when it does, recognize it, and make sure you stick with it.

How Advertising Works: Why Fame Is More Important Than Persuasion

As a brand manager on Surf Excel some fifteen years ago, I would eagerly wait to see the impact of every new ad we made on sales. While most of the time nothing happened, I did notice a pattern in the successful ads we made.

On our 'mind measure market research' where we asked consumers every month what they thought of our brands, a measure called Spontaneous Awareness (SPONT) would be most sensitive to good advertising. When asked to name some detergents, if 50 of every 100 people said Surf Excel, the baseline SPONT of Surf Excel would be 50. When we ran good advertising, we would see this measure move up to, say, 55, and then sales growth would follow. Good advertising made you more famous, and fame, also called salience, drove sales.

Several subsequent studies within Unilever and of course Byron Sharp's *How Brands Grow* confirmed this early practical understanding of mine. The theory is as follows. **The consumer doesn't change the brand she mainly uses but is quite open to changing the set of brands she infrequently uses depending on whether it is at the top of her mind.** You want a chocolate badly, your favourite Dairy Milk is not available so you buy a Five Star which you saw an ad of yesterday (even though you may not remember you saw it). The interesting thing is that the overwhelming bulk of the purchases in every category are actually the infrequent ones.

If salience is so important in driving sales, how does one make salient advertising? The HUL way believes there are two factors – enjoyment and branding. Of the two, enjoyment is the more important. It doesn't mean that you laugh when you see an ad. You simply must like seeing it again and again. So **the heart of advertising is making ads that people like to see.**

However, if people like to see the ad, but attribute it to some other brand, it serves no purpose. So branding is also important. But branding is not whether consumers recognize the brand logo. Quite the opposite. Good branding is being able to recognize the brand in the absence of the logo.

Callow brand managers fight with advertising agencies to put the brand logo on the top left of every frame or increase the size of the font. It either goes unnoticed by consumers or, worse, affects enjoyment. Think of the 44 ads in the picture on p. 67. Was a logo necessary to identify the brand? For an ad to drive salience it must be enjoyable and build on the associations a brand enjoys.

While salience is generally more important in advertising, persuasion does have a role. You must usually persuade a consumer to enter a new category like green tea or hair conditioners or dish-wash liquid. But even in persuasive advertising, enjoyment and branding are important to get people's attention. It is just a question of priority.

How to Brief the 'Mad Men' and Women

It is not vital that the creative person should identify with the business target – and creatives do tend to be uninterested in it – though it helps. In general, it is better not to clutter the creative's mind with your business woes. Broadly, creatives want to understand two things: who they should speak to and what they should say.

The latter should ideally be one sentence, if not just a word. When it comes to who they should talk to, it is not useful to say '25–40-year-old women living in town, class 1–10 lakh, consuming Brooke Bond Red Label occasionally'. Instead try this: 'Women who are unafraid to take the first step in building human relations.' The creative person will automatically find someone they know who resembles this person and will make communication for that one bullseye target.

An ad can do one of two things: it can be either eyecatching/attention-grabbing/memorable and drive salience, for example, Brooke Bond or Surf Excel, or extremely persuasive like Dove or Lipton Green Tea. If you are focused on salience you need to get a cracker of an insight. The insight is of course the heart of the brief. *A contradiction obvious in hindsight.*

For instance, 'common ground is a cup away' is a great insight for a tea brief. On the other hand, if you want to be persuasive, which is advisable only when you are building a category, you need a very compelling proposition or a promise. *'Use Indulekha oil and grow back your hair in 4 weeks.'* A simple way of remembering this is that if you want to be remembered (as you should most of the time), empathize with your customer, but if you want to persuade her, then formulate a sharp and relevant promise.

The advertising legend Piyush Pandey recalls a brief he received in the early 1990s for a new soap that HUL was planning to launch called Le Sancy. Le Sancy was designed to be a soap that didn't get as mushy as regular soaps. The brief was a manual on how to make advertising on Le Sancy based on a successful launch in Chile twenty years ago.

The not-so-brief 'brief' contained everything from the size of the font to the TV script to which mediums must be chosen for advertising. But there were two things Piyush noticed. Print as a medium was left out of the guidelines and a sentence hidden in the mumbo jumbo saying 'Quality that lasts and lasts'. He created what he says is one of his favourite print ads. A regular soap called

Le Soggy that had melted in the water and the Le Sancy soap next to it with 'Le Sancy' written below. The tag line was of course 'Quality that lasts and lasts'. He says instead of the manual all he needed was that single line.

Keep the brief memorable, insightful and, most importantly, BRIEF.

The Goosebump Test

Consumers judge ads emotionally. Even the most scientific advertisements like those of toilet cleaners create an emotion of, say, raising a fear and then calming it. The trick to judging a script or a finished ad is to be sensitive to your emotional response.

Does it elicit a smile, a lump in the throat, does the hair on your skin rise, is there a tingle in the belly? To say that the ad will work for the target but not for me or vice versa is a cop-out. All human beings are similar and great creative output like *Sholay* works for everyone. Taste is often a matter of prejudice. The ads in the illustration on p. 67 – Surf Excel, Zoozoos, the Google Indo-Pak ads – were liked by everyone.

The Greek historian Herodotus said that when the Persians had to make a decision, they first made it when they were drunk and then made it again when they were sober. The decision had to be the same both times for it to be taken.

Once you get an intuitive 'go / no go' for an ad film, then put on your thinking cap again. Ask a few basic questions. Are the feelings the script evoked the ones you intended? Is the role of the brand integral to the film? Can you articulate the advertising idea easily? If the script passes the goosebump test and the answers to these three questions are yes, like the Persians you are good to go.

For an executive working with a creative, there is one cardinal rule. Do not play the role of a creative and try to fix scripts yourself. Accept or reject. Tell them what you felt when you saw the ad. But do not suggest fixes. Give the advertising agency the problem and not the solution. It is important not to demotivate the agency with harsh feedback. It is a labour of love and you have to be always open to the fact that you may not have got it right.

Equally, don't get coerced into not expressing what you feel. Sometimes the agency will bring several people including very senior people into the room in an attempt to intimidate you. But if you don't feel anything at the end of the script reading, you should say it. This isn't just my advice for any business working with advertisement agencies – keep this as your cardinal rule as a professional working with any kind of creative.

At HUL judgement doesn't stop simply at approving a script. As I said before, HUL accounts for roughly 15 per cent of the country's ad spends on TV. Getting an ad wrong is extremely costly. After the script is approved it goes through – you guessed it – rigorous consumer work.

First the script is read to a few consumers to see if they like it and understand it. The script then gets made into an animatic or a cartoon and is then quantitatively tested with consumers on a few key questions – is it enjoyable, is it branded and is it persuasive? The questions are on a 5-point scale and the scores are indexed with a database. It is considered a green light if it hits the top two-thirds of the database. In salience- or fame-type ads I tend to push for the ad to be in the top 10 per cent of the database on branding and enjoyment. In market development–type films, I push for it to be in top 10 per cent on persuasion.

Producing Great Advertising: What's the Backstory

Production is the final stop in the advertising process. If the creative agency is the architect of the house, the director of the film is the mason. She actually builds it. The agency should have a free hand in choosing the director once you have finalized the costs. But have a look at the showreel of the director before approving the choice. In my experience, there are three kinds of directors – those who get emotions, those who get humour and those who shoot beautifully. Choose the director on the basis of what you want the ad to be like.

The director will often look at the film slightly differently and you must be flexible in incorporating her idea while still being true to the script that was tested. A meeting called the PPM or pre-production meeting is the forum where HUL, the agency and the director meet to discuss how the script will be treated while being shot. Typically, the director will give her version of the film, show you the cast, the costumes, the locations and the music.

PPMs can either pass quickly, with the client having no view on anything, or degenerate into silly conversations on whether the dress should be dark blue or light blue. **The best PPMs are those where you have detailed conversations with the director on how she sees the characters in the film. What sort of people are they likely to be, what were they doing the same day before the events of the film unfolded? Also get an understanding of what in the film excites the director. Is it the same thing that excites the consumers?** Once you are aligned on the soul of the film and the character of the actors, the director will do a much better job than you in selecting costumes, actors, music and sets. Let her.

In general, if the PPM is good, **it is usually a bad idea for the client to go for the shoot, and HUL discourages it.** That is back-seat driving and often ends in an accident. When the final film is shown to you, react the way you should have when the script was read to you. Does it evoke any sensation in you? Treat it like you would after a meal has been served in an expensive restaurant. Add a bit of salt or pepper if you must, but don't ask the chef to change the dish according to your taste. If the food doesn't work for you, bear it with a philosophical grin. Likewise, while you can make minor changes to a film after it has been produced, there's little you can do if it has fundamentally not worked out. The right course of action if the film doesn't work is not to air it on TV. No point putting good money behind bad.

Two Case Studies: Surf Excel and Lifebuoy

Let me now write about two case studies that illustrate the points I have been making above. In one I had only a ring-side view, while in the other I was in the arena. The Lifebuoy case is a great example of advertising strategy while the Surf Excel one is much more on advertising execution. By the way, both had the same advertising leader, Gopal Vittal, currently CEO of Airtel and one of the best advertising minds in the country.

Like all sales managers in the early 2000s, I regarded Lifebuoy as the lifeline of HUL. More people in India used Lifebuoy than had electricity in those days. Unfortunately, in those days Lifebuoy was in terminal decline. The market was offering better products at lower prices and consumers were leaving the age-old health promise of Lifebuoy in droves. HUL planned a relaunch of Lifebuoy – Project Butterfly – in 2002. It was a hush-hush project, but there were rumours that the iconic carbolic fragrance of the soap was to be changed, the quality was to be improved and the price too was to be dramatically taken up.

Hardly the right solution, we sales chaps thought, for a brand in distress. But at the launch conference Gopal explained the rationale of the launch. He showed us the most famous Lifebuoy ad from the 1980s. Mazhar Khan playing hockey to the background music of '*Lifebuoy hai jahan, tandurusti hai wahan*' (to watch it, search for Lifebuoy Mazhar Khan on YouTube).

We were a famous brand that consumers didn't have a strong reason to buy. A generic masculine health claim was not persuasive to the real consumer – low-income rural women. Instead, he said, the problem that Lifebuoy solves is that of preventing children from falling ill due to germs. Rural women didn't know what germs were since they were invisible and therefore didn't connect them to their children falling ill. Educating them was the task.

He then showed us an ad where a doctor visits a house where a young boy is lying sick. As he goes to wash his hands he notices that the soap in the basin is an ordinary soap and not Lifebuoy. He tells the boy's mother that he is sick because of invisible germs that would have got killed had she used Lifebuoy. I still get goose bumps when I see this ad (search for Lifebuoy Butterfly Stomach Infection on YouTube). Not because it was a particularly creative ad, but because it was such a radical yet rigorous departure from the brand codes.

As can be expected at the end of a story like this, Lifebuoy turned around and everyone lived happily ever after. But the real marketing lesson is to take a brand that was using salience- or fame-driven marketing in an established category like soap and convert it to persuasion-led marketing. This sounds contrary to the point I made earlier saying that for winning shares in established categories one must be salient and not persuasive. But what Lifebuoy was trying to do here was to use an established format (bar soap) to create a new subcategory of germ protection. It was category development all right, just masked in the oldest category of all: soap.

A second example is from Surf. By late 2005 I had spent three years as a brand manager on Surf Excel. We had tried every trick in the advertising book for five years – removes chocolate stains, removes ink stains, removes every stain, removes stains without fading colour and removes stains in half the time. We had also done several share-price-bruising price drops. But none of it was growing the brand.

A few years earlier we had tried to adapt a Brazilian campaign called Modern Parenting which told parents that stains were a part of learning and that children should be encouraged to get dirty. We used examples of art and cycling, but mums told us that they felt art and cycling were fun, not educational. Stains were accidental, at most incidental, but certainly not providential. It was unacceptable for mothers to encourage their children to get dirty. Gopal joined the laundry category in 2005 as my boss's boss and felt that there was something in the Brazilian idea that we needed to adapt to India. Fresh from his Lifebuoy experiences, Gopal nudged me in the direction of values. Values, he said, were the only thing that mums placed above academic learning.

When I met consumers, I realized that Gopal was right. Mums did cherish values like empathy, expressing love and generosity over learning, especially the value of expressing love. But I also realized that as children grow, they tend not to tell their mothers about their everyday experiences and their soiled clothes tell the actual story. Most importantly, mums were able to relate with the fact that usually children display values through actions and not words and this involves getting dirty.

We gave the ace creatives R. Balki, Priti Nair and Arun Iyer from Lintas (now Lowe Lintas) the following brief.

Target audience: Mums who cherish the values of curiosity, creativity, a sense of community, a desire to succeed and emotional bonding (with mums) in their children.

81

Insight: Mums are curious to know about their child's experiences and they never cease to be amazed.

Main point: Behind every stain is a beautiful story!

Gopal added the 'beautiful' word to the line 'Behind every stain is a story' minutes before the briefing. We did several rounds of script hearing sessions, but nothing clicked. The films weren't beautiful enough. Then one day Gopal called me at around 11 p.m. and asked me to come to Olive restaurant in Bandra. Lintas had cracked a few scripts and Balki was rushing down to share them with us. Balki narrated three scripts. I forget the first, but the second was about a boy who sees a pipe leaking and pedestrians doing nothing about it. He jumps in and tries his best to close the pipe and in the process gets dirty. The third story, which we finally chose, was about a boy and his sister walking back home from school, when his sister falls in a puddle. To stop her from crying the boy jumps into the puddle and gets into a mock fight with it.

The film was directed beautifully by Abhinay Deo, who later directed the black comedy *Delhi Belly*. At the PPM Abhinay insisted on the concept of 'clean dirt' in contrast to 'filth' and we set the film in a sylvan hill station where the mud looks clean enough to roll in. When we aired the ad, we instantly saw electricity on the brand. Awareness measures shot up, as did sales. I recall a woman talking to

me about the ad with tears in her eyes. Her own brother
and she were estranged. How she wished her son would
be to her daughter in later years as the brother and sister
were in the ad.

The Puddle ad (search for Surf Excel Puddlewar on
YouTube) went on to be the first in a series of 'Daag
achhe hain' – dirt is good – campaigns, which the *Economic
Times* called among the top ten campaigns of the decade
2000–10. The ad is featured in the 2019 picture with
44 of India's most famous ads. Most importantly, Surf,
which was HUL's fifth largest brand in 2005, is today
HUL's largest brand.

The 'dirt is good' campaign is a great example of taking
a category that everyone knows about (laundry), a brand
whose benefit also everyone knows about (stain removal)
and then converting it from boring, functional advertising
trying to be persuasive into advertising that really becomes
famous and drives sales.

Great advertising is a secret sauce for success that only
a few can master, and hence it is a competitive advantage.
But even more important than the quality of advertising is
getting your message across to as many people as quickly
as possible. In other words, good media planning and
deployment. Let us talk about a few key principles of
media planning.

Media Planning: Whispering to Many Is Better Than Shouting to a Few

At our village in Etah during my rural training stint, school was in a large harvested sugar cane field. Each class from JKG to second standard sat at a short distance from each other. The sole teacher, Manoharlal Yadavji, would walk cane in hand from one class to the other shouting a lesson for each class to repeat till he came back. Caning was a random activity intended more as an exciting break from the monotony of repetition than as a deterrent. The back rows of the class, the main recipients of the canings, could scarcely hear him but would quickly catch up by copying the students in front. When explaining media reach to students and younger marketeers, I use a made-up story from this unforgettable experience.

What if Yadavji had to announce that there would be no school tomorrow but his voice was so hoarse that he could say it only four times. Would he say it four times to the same class? If so, 100 per cent of one class would hear the announcement, but the other three classes wouldn't hear him at all. Of the total, 25 per cent of the students would have got the message. On the other hand, if he said it once to each class, the back row students wouldn't have heard it, but 80 per cent of each class and hence 80 per cent of the whole school would have got the message:

25 per cent versus 80 per cent message reach based on different media strategies.

There is not much else to understand in media planning apart from this. Reach more people a fewer number of times than reach fewer people more times or more impactfully.

Vipul Mathur, a former Lifebuoy brand manager, recalls flying with a colleague from Thiruvananthapuram to Mumbai. The colleague had just read *How Brands Grow* and they were chatting about the 'mental reach' or percentage of consumers reached with any message of a large brand like Lifebuoy every month. Vipul realized that Lifebuoy was spending all its money on television, fragmenting it over four or five ads. Each ad was reaching about 40 per cent of TV viewers and it was also reaching the same set of heavy TV users. So if one TV ad reached 40 per cent of people, five reached not much more. Maybe 45 per cent. Given that only about half of Lifebuoy users owned a TV, effectively Lifebuoy was giving four or five messages three or four times a month to about 23 per cent of its users. Vipul simplified the media plan, cutting ads on air to only two, and reinvesting the money saved into mediums like wall paintings and print which reached consumers not reached by TV. Media reach and growth both grew exponentially.

The fundamental currency in media planning is reach

and frequency (how many times you reach a person). It is clear from the above examples that reach must *always* be prioritized over frequency or impact.

A corollary to the principle of reach widely is to not over-segment. Nine out of ten times we make mistakes in defining a target group too narrowly for media planning. We define it based on who we assume is the target group. For instance, for many years on Cornetto ice cream we defined the target group as teenagers when actually it was being consumed by everyone from ages six to eighty. Yes, teenagers were consuming about 20 per cent more than others, but our ultra-sharp targeting meant we were spending four to five times more money on reaching a teenager when the benefit was just a little more.

Most messages are relevant to almost *everybody*.

Whisper to everybody rather than shout to a chosen few.

Selects Mediums Based on Cost and Not Rhetoric

There is a lot of voodoo regarding which media to spend money on. Some people believe that a particular medium is more premium than the other or better suits the brand. This is a brand that works on TV or my brand is so premium that it will only work on the back pages of the *Cosmopolitan* magazine. Evidence for 'media as message' is thin and using basic economics makes most sense.

Say you want to reach *all* Indians with a message of 'Always use a condom while having sex' (sex, along with dogs and babies, is the easiest way to grab attention in advertising). TV is by far the most low cost scale medium in the country. With about Rs 4 crore you will reach 40 per cent of the TV viewing households (approximately 200 million of a total of 280 million households) in the country or about 80 million households. The thing about TV is that some people watch a lot of it but many more watch little. It is easy to reach heavy viewers but tough to reach the lighter viewers. So you realize that the next Rs 1 crore gets you only 3 per cent more or 6 million viewers.

Do you continue with TV? You scout around for the various media – print, cinema, radio – to see what you can do with Rs 1 crore. You see that a Rs 1 crore print plan can get you a readership of 10 million households. Much better than the 6 million extra unsafe souls on TV? Not really. Of the 10 million print households, only 1 million don't own a TV and of the 9 million who do, 60 per cent haven't seen your ad (you have reached 40 per cent of TV households, remember?). So for Rs 1 crore you get 1 million + 60 per cent of 9 million = 6.4 million households. Better, but just slightly better, than the 6 million households you can get from TV. You need to continue this process till you run out of money or arrive at your reach target.

As you can see there is no better or worse medium for a message. Just a cheaper and more expensive one depending on your objectives.

Swarnim Bharadwaj, a former brand manager on Lux, recalls 'constantly being on the hunt for incremental reach, we sometimes had fortuitous results in other areas. Average TV cost per person reached used to be about Re 1. Print, outdoor media and radio, all had higher cost but became useful only after TV stopped delivering incremental reach. At this point I was approached by a vendor selling cinema advertising [the ads that play before your movie starts]. At first what seemed to be a small medium turned out to be quite substantial with over 6000 single screens and 2000 multiplexes available. Moreover, they could be split neatly by state, language and city tier to deliver targeted ads. While it wasn't incremental reach over the TV medium, the cherry on the cake turned out to be the low cost at only 30 paise per person reached (on a giant screen with undivided attention). So even if 50 per cent of the people had already seen the ad on TV, for the balance 50 per cent who owned a TV but hadn't seen the ad the cost was only 60 paise. Much cheaper than other media. We realized how brands like Vicco Turmeric had been milking this medium successfully for years and we quickly followed suit. If you frequent cinema halls, you will now notice the slew of Unilever ads there today . . . apologies!'

Ashwin Moorthy, a former brand manager on Lifebuoy Handwash, recalls how good reach planning requires consumer intimacy and creativity. He says, 'In 2010 all TV media planning was founded on TAM data, an urban panel–based TV measurement tool. TAM data was never questioned and was then the only industry standard. However, in the beginning of 2011, a group of skin cleansing managers visited dozens of consumers in rural central India and came back with a consistent observation: the channels that featured in TAM-based planning weren't the ones rural consumers viewed the most. Free to air channels like Start Utsav and Dangal had by that time completely disrupted Doordarshan, and rural consumers now had access to high quality programming for free. Of course, urban consumers who paid cable TV fees didn't watch these channels and hence TAM never reported them as high reach drivers. So a large supply of spots on these channels were then cheaply available. We lapped up this inventory for our rural portfolio, primarily Lux and Lifebuoy. While in TAM terms we were technically delivering less reach, we allowed consumer insight and marketing common sense to rule. All this was of course validated nearly a decade later when the industry caught up. The newly established BARC panel, now capturing rural, revealed these channels to be among the top five watched in the country. And of course, our brands strengthened in the period, at a significant cost advantage.'

Now that we have understood the sexiest part of business – advertising – let us move to its most important part – the product – in the next chapter.

But before that let us summarize why mastery of advertising and media makes HUL managers an obvious choice as CMOs across industries.

Summary

1. Communication is a critical competitive advantage in any business.
2. Be clear on who you are. Reinforce this in every piece of communication.
3. Being remembered is much more important than being persuasive.
4. Brief creatives simply, memorably, insightfully and most important briefly.
5. Do a goosebump test (how do you feel) while judging creative output.
6. Share your understanding of a film with the director and then give her the freedom to execute.
7. Better to whisper to many than shout to a few.
8. Don't over-segment. Buyers are far more widespread than you think.
9. Take economics-driven and not ideological positions on media.

4

Get the Product Right, the Brand Will Follow

Product Development Lessons from Hindustan Unilever

In 1999 as a management trainee I was visiting Katni, a town north of Jabalpur in Madhya Pradesh, with my sales officer (my boss) to launch Kissan jam sachets. Mishraji would go from shop to shop, tear the sachet, squeeze half of it into his own mouth, thrust the other half into the shopkeeper's mouth and say, *'Chatni se meetha hai na?'* (Isn't it sweeter than chutney?) He told me that all you had to say in your sales pitch was that Dalda should taste like ghee, ketchup should taste better than tomato chatni and jam should be sweeter than a sweet chatni.

Over the years I forgot Mishraji's lesson and had to rediscover why brands grow. There is a natural tendency to assume that the work one is doing is the most important thing in the world. I first thought that brands grow when you pack shops with them; a little later I veered to the view that wide distribution was the magic bullet. As I moved to marketing, I first thought great consumer promotions were the main thing. By my next more strategic job I was convinced it was advertising that was the answer. As I entered my first middle management role, I was sure it was pricing but as general manager soaps I was convinced that media was the answer. Now exactly twenty years later, with a broad-brush understanding of all functions, I find Mishraji's tutorial spot on. Get the product right and the rest will follow.

Take this book, for instance. If it is good, the other Ps of marketing – pricing, publicity, the cover and availability – will help. But if it is not interesting and useful to the reader, no matter how much publicity the publishers give it or how easily it is available in bookstores, it will not sell.

Product is the most important P in marketing. It is the most important P in business. That is why every CEO needs to be the chief product officer as well.

Blockbusters vs Product Evolution

Dr Vibhav Sanzgiri, currently R&D director at HUL, recounts the story of the birth of HUL's blockbuster brand Fair & Lovely. Fair & Lovely had its roots in HUL's infant nutrition business that was subsequently sold. The team was working on solutions to vitamin B3 deficiency among children. The absence of niacinamide, a form of vitamin B3, leads to pellagra, which causes dark patches on the skin. While looking for solutions in foods, one of the scientists, G.S Mathur, asked if pellagra could be treated by topically applying niacinamide on the skin.

HUL scientists looked at young tadpoles when pigmentation starts to develop on tails that are transparent at birth. When they applied niacinamide they saw that the pigmentation would reduce and when they put the tadpoles back into water the pigmentation would reappear. By coating the dark patches with vitamin B3 they were able to temporarily revert to the birth colour of the tadpole.

Mathur then took niacinamide and mixed it with a basic vanishing cream to create the famous Fair & Lovely. Vibhav says Fair & Lovely is a natural way to get the skin back to the tone that you were born with, which with heat, stress and lack of vitamin B3 has become a few shades darker.

This is the kind of blockbuster innovation that is celebrated in books and management schools. Companies invest billions of dollars to try to get innovations such as these. But blockbusters require luck. The interesting thing in the Fair & Lovely story is not the innovation but the company culture that enabled it. Equally interesting are the many non-blockbuster, evolutionary product innovations that create as much if not more value.

Let's take the laundry category. In the last hundred years there have been three fundamental product innovations that have improved cleaning – the introduction of bleach in soap powder, the replacement of vegetable-oil-based washing powder with petrochemical-based ones and the introduction of enzymes as an aid in stain removal.

We have had several more innovations that have improved the washing experience – liquid detergents that aid in solubility, detergents that overcome the problem of cleaning in hard water and low lathering detergents that don't foam out of your washing machines. There has been a third set of innovations, which look minor but have created massive value: multicoloured speckles in detergent powders that improve perception of clean, encapsulated fragrances that bloom while clothes are getting washed and density changes in your washing powder that can cue either economy or power.

The important thing in product development is not to obsess about the revolutionary nature of change in a product but to focus on understanding and fulfilling consumer needs. That is where value is created. Product development has five components: understand the consumer need in depth, create a product and innovation culture in the company, test before you launch, persist patiently and, finally, obsess about delivered product quality.

Understanding Consumer Needs

The starting point of all great product development is consumer insight. My boss Hanneke Faber, president of Unilever's Foods and Refreshments division, recently told me that while managers focus on solutions, entrepreneurs obsess on the consumer problem.

One of the things that Aart Weijburg noticed in the early 2000s was that HUL was not particularly good at consumer connectedness, especially in rural markets. When HUL managers travelled to rural areas it was to visit shops and the few times they visited consumers they went in the afternoon by which time the villagers were done with the bulk of their chores.

'Get me to the village when the sun rises. I am happy if it means camping outside the village in a tent for the night,' Aart told his team. I think the team told him that India was not quite Holland yet and a big Dutchman camping outside a village may not be the most unobtrusive thing on earth. Nonetheless the point was made and Aart started visiting villages at 6 a.m., when women bathe, wash their clothes and cook food.

He recalls one visit he made to a village in northern Maharashtra with the head of Unilever Home Care's R&D function. As they entered the village, they saw a tanker filling a dry well. In the village, they saw a woman smearing cow dung on the floors and walls of her house. When they asked her why, she said it was to keep flies away. It was counter-intuitive to the Western mind that poo can keep flies away and that it has long been an Indian practice.

When he started speaking to consumers, Aart realized that the single biggest problem they were facing was diarrhoea-related deaths. The causes for diarrhoea were drinking unclean water, not washing hands with soap after defecation and flies. Aart says that this one visit gave him the bulk of the consumer innovation ideas for the next five years. A detergent that lathered less and so could save water, a handwash awareness programme on Lifebuoy, cleaner water through Pureit water purifiers and a project in partnership with SC Johnson to keep flies away. The first three have been very successful for HUL but even Aart and HUL have not succeeded in keeping flies away in India.

Just as Aart's product insights came up by changing the consumer lens from visits in the afternoon to visits in the early morning, there are ways in which you can analyse data differently to get a great product idea.

A few years ago, when Himanshu Kanwar, currently general manager for ice creams, was brand manager, Brooke Bond, he came up with the thesis that to win leadership in tea nationally you only had to win very deep in a few sociocultural regions (SCRs). Using the criteria of size of opportunity and ability of HUL to win, he identified five SCRs, including coastal Andhra Pradesh, that were must-win battles. When he looked closer at coastal Andhra Pradesh, he realized that while our market share in larger packs was the same as that of the competitor, in small packs it was only one-fifth.

In a brilliant piece of detective work, Himanshu identified that even in small packs the penetration or number of users for Brooke Bond and the competitor was the same but the consumption per household was much less for Brooke Bond. When he came to me with this odd piece of data, I told him, as I have explained previously in the book, that while penetration is usually driven by awareness and distribution, consumption is driven by price and product quality.

Since the price of Brooke Bond and its competitor was the same, there was likely an issue with the product. Himanshu excitedly came back the next day and said that the Brooke Bond blend on the smaller pack was of poorer quality than the larger pack. A decade ago, it had been decided that poorer consumers weren't willing to pay for high quality and to hold prices in inflationary times had cut the quality of the blend. Despite a mandate from the company a few years later that large packs and small packs should have the same formulation, this particular blend had slipped through the cracks.

Himanshu and I boarded the next available flight to Vijayawada. In a town called Samarlakota near Vijayawada we met a shopkeeper who told us that Brooke Bond was meant for high-class people, but labour class wanted stronger tea.

Given that richer consumers buy the larger pack and poorer consumers the sachet, he was alluding to the difference in quality between the two packs. We then drove through verdant fields towards Rajahmundry.

At Anaparti village we disembarked to meet a woman called P. Satyavathi. The one-pager on Satyavathi that market research had given us said that her husband was a 'mission operator'. Half expecting to enter a church, we found that Satyavathi's husband, apart from being a mechanic, was the owner of two prized cocks that had won several trophies at cockfights. While watching a cockfight, we asked Satyavathi to make two cups of tea for us: one with Brooke Bond sachets and the other with the sachets of our competitor.

The difference in colour and strength was chalk and cheese. After some polite conversation on which was the better cock (the better tea was obvious), we left, answer in hand. HUL's additional investment in Brooke Bond sachets in Andhra Pradesh, to match it to the large pack, has yielded amazing results in market shares.

Great pieces of consumer understanding can come from strange places. A while ago I was reading *Early*

Which is the better cock? Which is the better tea?

Indians by Tony Joseph. The book uses the latest genetic evidence to piece together who our ancestors were. Joseph talks about a gene mutation called 13910T which originated in Europe about 7500 years ago and which allows humans to digest lactose present in milk. Large population swathes of North and West India have this mutant gene while equally large numbers in the East and South don't have this gene and are hence lactose intolerant. He makes a further argument – that since people in the North and West get their protein through milk, they tend to be vegetarian and those in the South and East tend to be non-vegetarian. Suddenly several puzzles on the eating habits of people in the subcontinent which had gnawed at my mind became clear.

A few weeks earlier, I had visited a village near Coimbatore and been surprised by the quantity and variety of meat in the diet of women there. Apart from chicken and fish, goat liver, partridge and quail were being consumed frequently. Contrast this with my visit in early 2019 to 'carnivorous' Pakistan, where a farmer near Multan told me their diet was predominantly vegetarian, with meat, due to its high price, being served once a week. I understood why the quality of teas sold in Punjab was poor (they merely needed a colour addition to thick milk), why Bengalis use desserts made of chhena (it has much less lactose), why Gujaratis eat so much ice cream made from dairy fat, while the Assamese prefer vegetable fat for theirs.

Great product insights come from everywhere: you just need to have a curious mind and the ability to make connections.

Create a Product Culture

In 1957 Steve Turner, then chairman of HUL, set up the first R&D laboratory for Unilever outside the Western world. The Hindustan Lever Research Centre (HLRC), as it was known, was also the first major R&D centre of a multinational in India. Before this, products that had been developed in Western labs were either sold as they were or in the best case watered down and sold at lower prices in the developing world. Turner foresaw the impending shortage in the traditional oils that were used in making soap and felt the need to upgrade less-known indigenous oils like rice bran and castor to a quality suitable for making soap. But fundamental scientific advances and a laboratory would be needed for this.

Over the years HUL's R&D set-up has come up with some world-class innovations that have travelled well beyond the shores of India – from detergent bars to Fair & Lovely to Vim Bar to, most recently, Pureit water purifiers.

Priya Nair, executive director, Home Care, recalls the launch of Rin Nil Mineral Bar as a great example of HUL R&D's prowess. Rin, which is synonymous with detergent bars, was facing stiff competition from cheaper bars in the late 1990s and early 2000s. There wasn't much to differentiate it from mass bars, and consumers didn't think the price premium was worth it. While the main cleaning agents in a detergent bar are surfactants (derivatives of petroleum), minerals are used to structure the bar and keep it neither too hard nor too soggy. The minerals however give the bars a dull look and if you have used a bar to wash clothes you will have seen these grit particles rubbing on to the clothes and your hands.

Around the turn of the century scientists in HUL had patented a way to structure bars without minerals. The resultant bar was a lot brighter and smoother to use but didn't really clean any better. Priya talks about the dilemma the team faced. We had a patented product that had just a few benefits but necessitated heavy capital investment in the factory. Would the trade-off be worth it? Finally, the team launched the Rin Nil Mineral Bar with many small consumer perceptible benefits as add-ons.

The bar was duster-shaped instead of cuboid, which made it more ergonomic, a flow wrap packaging against the norm of paper packaging in the industry made it more modern and a brighter blue colour enhanced its clean perception. The product was launched with a simple proposition of 'No Mitti' or 'No Mud'. Fifteen years later a brand that was declining in its worst year by minus 25 per cent has given a compound growth of 10 per cent over the period and is the undisputed leader in the massive detergent bar market.

But investment in R&D is only one way to create an innovation or products culture. The more important way is to get the entire organization obsessed with products.

One of the big benefits of creating a culture of entrepreneurial professionals is that everyone in every part of the business knows about the other parts of the businesses. By structurally ensuring that manufacturing people spend time in R&D and vice versa, HUL has an R&D team that has great commercial acumen and some of its marketing people have a great understanding of R&D. It is absolutely critical that business people understand the underlying science of how their products work and it is actually quite simple once you structure your thoughts.

Products contain ingredients that have certain attributes, and these attributes give certain benefits. When you work on a business you have to draw a simple table to list these three and understand how they work. Let us take tea, for instance – what benefits do you seek from it? It must wake you up, it has a sensorial factor of taste and smell that is pleasurable and it must do these without hurting the purse strings. The awakening or stimulating benefit of tea is driven by an attribute called strength which in turn is driven by its caffeine content. The sensorial aspects of tea are driven by the attributes of taste and aroma which in turn are driven by the volatiles and polyphenols it contains. The economy of tea usage is driven by the speed of infusion and the darkness of colour which are in turn driven by particle size and how well the tea is oxidized in the factory. So to understand the essence of tea you can draw a table like the one on p. 106.

Essence of Tea

Benefit	Attribute	Driving Ingredient
Wakes me up	Strength	Caffeine content
Lovely sensorial experience	Aroma	Volatiles
	Taste	Polyphenols
Must be economical to use	Speed of infusion	Particle size
	Colour	Oxidation

Once you have understood this fundamental for a category, you need to understand the interlinkages between ingredients and how you can manipulate them to get a desired end. In this case while smaller particle size gives you faster infusion, it also means that more volatiles have escaped the leaf before reaching your pan. This is so because smaller particle size means more surface area (to see if this is true, you can calculate the surface area of a barfi, then break it into two and measure the surface area again), which gives more space for volatiles to escape.

Poorer consumers are willing to compromise on the sensorial benefits providing they get their 'wake me up' delivered economically. Hence in general, but not always, dust teas tend to be cheaper than leaf teas and that is also why your neighbourhood tea stall tea looks very different from what you drink at home.

What if you are a consumer, like in Tamil Nadu, who wants a strong cup but also tea aroma and taste? A smaller particle size will guarantee strength but will have less aroma. The trick is to get a tea that is high in volatiles and polyphenols so that despite small particle size it continues to have the right aroma. In a tea bush, the leaf bud and the first two leaves below the leaf bud have the most volatiles and polyphenols. So if you pluck tea very fine so that only two leaves and a leaf bud are plucked you will have tea that is very high in volatile content. You can now powder it into dust and it will give you strength and flavour. HUL's incredibly strong brand in Tamil Nadu, 3Roses, is a great example of this principle.

Understanding benefits, attributes and ingredients is an important mental formulation in designing products and removing avoidable costs. The vast majority of consumers want benefits and are not interested in ingredients. Sometimes they demand ingredients, and product developers add these ingredients even though they have better ways to deliver the benefits. For example, when consumers say they want buttery cookies they mean they want cookies that taste buttery, and a product may add a few percentage points of butter just to substantiate the claim. Then again there are products like our hair oil Indulekha, which is clinically proven to increase hair growth but all we know is that it has an ancient Ayurvedic ingredient. Srirup Mitra, who worked closely on the brand, talks about how the product uses a potent mix of Ayurveda and Siddha with a seven-day natural sunlight maturation. Ingredient-led product development works sometimes, but mostly it is still benefit-led R&D that works.

Test, Test and Test Again

There is a tendency to believe, with Apple being the poster child of the belief, that consumers don't know what they really want till they actually see a breakthrough product in the market. In practice this is the exception and not the rule. Rigorous testing of products is absolutely essential 90 per cent of the time.

In 2008 when Paul Polman became the CEO of Unilever, he insisted that all brands blind-test their product with the competitor's product. A blind test is one in which consumers are given a product without the brand name and packaging and asked to rate it on a list of attributes including overall opinion. A similar set (but not the same) of consumers are given the competitor's products and asked to rate it as well. For a blind win our brand has to significantly beat the score of the competitor's product on overall opinion.

When HUL started blind-testing its products, it was shocked to realize that a vast majority of products were blind parity, that is, consumers could not really tell the difference between two products. A flurry of activity started to achieve the stated goal of '60 per cent win in blind-testing'. I remember washing clothes with scores of consumers in small towns and villages with our bottom-of-the-pyramid brand Wheel. Two things we noticed were that in their small wash areas women valued fragrance a lot more than urban consumers who used washing machines. Second, in dimly lit bathrooms, a whiter-looking powder was more starkly visible and cued efficacy. By improving the fragrance and making the powder whiter, Wheel was able to achieve a blind win.

Quantitative testing is not a substitute for getting a real feel with consumers. In fact, the more senior you are the more important it is to be close to consumers. HUL was considering buying Indulekha, an Ayurvedic hair oil sold in South India that promised to reduce hair fall. Sanjiv Mehta, the current chairman of HUL, recalls visiting twenty-five consumers over three days to understand consumer perception of the brand. He met users who were delighted with the product. With trepidation he next met consumers who had used the brand but had given it up. When he asked them why they had stopped using the brand they told him that it was so good that their hair fall problem had entirely stopped. They had no real need to use it any more. Sanjiv gave a green signal and a brand that HUL bought for Rs 330 crore in 2015 is now worth Rs 2000 crore.

Persist Patiently

Product breakthroughs happen much slower than is commonly believed. In one hundred years of the detergent powder industry there have been no more than three or four significant product breakthroughs. Once you are on to a product idea, you must be extremely patient in seeing it through.

Scouring powders used to wash dishes in the early 1990s were not a very economical solution. Used in fistfuls, a lot of it tended to get washed down the drain without even touching a vessel. More so, consumers complained, when maids washed the dishes. The idea of making the powder into a bar which guaranteed much more economy of use had been around for at least ten years. But HUL could never get it right – sometimes the bar would be too hard; sometimes it would get too soggy. After the fourth failed attempt, Nitin Paranjpe, then brand manager, recollects that Vindi Banga, director detergents, wrote in the margins of the report: 'This has been tested to death, it is time to bury it.' The project was closed down. Around this time the R&D manager on the project, Winston

Pereira, told Nitin that he felt he had solved the problem. He had got a bar that was neither too mushy nor too hard. Intrepidly, Nitin walked up to Vindi and asked for the project to be revived. Another expensive, time-consuming test would be needed. Given that projects are normally given at maximum three chances, Nitin isn't still clear why Vindi allowed the fifth and final test on Vim Bar. Vim Bar is now ubiquitously found across Indian kitchens.

The man credited with building the immensely profitable personal products business which now contributes to half of HUL's profits was V. Kasturirangan. Built like a rugby player, which he was, Kas inspired fear and adoration in his team. Legend has it that in the early days of building the shampoo sachet business, Kas would carry shampoo sachets in the bonnet of his car whenever he visited a market. If sachets were not seen in an outlet Kas would first place these for free in the shop before giving the area sales manager (ASM) a public dressing-down. Shahi Kalathil, the ASM of Bangalore, allegedly told Kas that despite trying hard, sachets were not selling, and it was perhaps time to withdraw them from the market. 'Young man, I would rather withdraw the ASM than the sachets from the market,' was KAS's characteristic reply.

It Is Delivered Quality and Not Design Quality That Matters

The quality of a product made in the lab may be different from that which is made in the factory which is different from what is bought at the shop which is different when the consumer uses the product. In the final analysis what matters is the consumer experience and it is important to ensure that there is no loss in translation between the laboratory and the moment a consumer uses the product.

When Aart Weijburg got to India in 1999, he noticed that compared to many Unilever companies, HUL had prioritized productivity and costs over quality. Aart says he made a mission of reinstating the belief in quality in the company and to that end spent time visiting factories and drilling this in.

On a visit to a soap factory, Aart took a soap bar out of the line and noticed a big dent on it. The petrified factory manager said it was an exception and to prove it pulled out a soap from the line which didn't have a dent. Aart then waited for two more minutes, pulled out a bar and saw another dent. He waited another two minutes, pulled out another bar and found this too had a dent on it.

Furious, he called a meeting of the factory managers and asked them to shut the line down till they solved the problem. 'But what about productivity?' squealed the factory manager. 'Stuff productivity. Quality is much, much more important,' retorted Aart. In this sombre moment, the production manager ran into the meeting and said they had identified the root cause of the problem.

It was Aart's large and powerful Dutch farmer thumb. Every time Aart touched the bar of soap, the pressure of his thumb was so intense that it would make a dent! Aart apologized profusely to the factory team but not without reinforcing that if a real dent were to be found, the factory must shut down regardless of the productivity consequences.

Sometime in early 2009 Wheel Bar got a blind product win on overall opinion over its competitor in blind-testing. I myself had taken the product to consumers and tested it with a competitor product. We were much better. There was much exultation in our team, and we were sure that the new product would win back market share. However, we soon realized that this blind win didn't make things better in the market; in fact it made it worse. Perplexed, I went back to consumers, this time buying the new Wheel Bar from the market. But now the new Wheel Bar was much worse. When we thought about it, we realized that the fragrance of the new Wheel Bar while powerful was designed to have strong top notes that gave a great whiff of fragrance but disappeared quite quickly. The blind test samples were taken straight from the factory and had much more fragrance than the eight-week-old ones we had bought from the market. Our perfume house had delivered on the brief on winning in the blind test but not in the market!

From product, we will next learn how HUL uses art and science in pricing.

But let us recap the lessons of this chapter which show the absolute criticality of the CEO and top management in product development.

Summary

1. Product is the most important P in marketing. Product obsession must start with the CEO.
2. For great product ideas get out of your comfort zone when interacting with consumers.
3. Good companies invest in R&D; in the best companies everyone is involved in R&D.
4. For every product, understand which ingredients deliver what attributes and what the benefits of each attribute are.
5. Does your product beat the competitor products when tested blind?
6. If you believe you are solving a real consumer problem with a great product, persist patiently.
7. What matters is the quality the consumer gets and not the quality you design in the laboratory.

5

The Art and Science of Pricing

Pricing Lessons from Hindustan Unilever

On a visit to the Gwalior wholesale market in February 2000, I observed that the trade prices of Lifebuoy and Lux soap were heavily discounted. I admonished the sales in charge of Gwalior, Chandu Joshi, for his poor control on prices. He said that this was an annual budget phenomenon, where wholesalers would buy Lifebuoy and Lux on credit from the HUL distributor, cut the price and sell it quickly at a loss. They would use the cash they got to stock up on ITC cigarettes in anticipation of the tax increase which was almost guaranteed in every budget. The old price cigarette stock could then be sold at a premium, which more than compensated for the loss they had made on soap.

This is just one example that shows how pricing in India is an incredibly complex field of business management. It is simultaneously an art and a science that is very difficult to master. Given its importance, in most companies CEOs are directly involved in pricing. The HUL approach to pricing offers some guidance but is in no way a definitive guide to pricing.

Price Discounts *Do Not* Recruit New Consumers

First let us look at how not to price. The biggest myth in pricing – practised by most e-commerce companies – is to 'price at a discount, recruit consumers and then take up the price'. Vindi Banga, former HUL chairman, took a very different view and is reported to have said, 'The gross margin a brand is born with is the gross margin that it dies with.'

What he meant is that while scale can improve net margin through advertising and overhead costs, gross margin or the difference between price and cost of material never structurally changes for a brand. Consumers use a brand for a quality at a certain price. If they come in at a low price and you take up prices, they will leave with the same velocity with which they entered.

This is true everywhere, but most apparent in Gujarat. My colleague V. Vijaygopal once told me that the Gujarati consumer has calculated the gross margins of all companies and selects the one that is lowest. Not the lowest price but the lowest gross margin. They are happy to pay a high price if the cost of raw material is equally high. In the early 2000s HUL launched Wheel Blue Bar to compete with Nirma in Gujarat. It was a product with great quality and an extremely affordable price, but made a gross margin of exactly zero per cent. The brand took off and rapidly became a challenger to Nirma. A few years later, having got scale, HUL felt that it was perhaps time to take up the price, but the moment we did so volumes collapsed. Hurriedly, we reverted to the old price. In 2008, when I was the marketing head for Wheel, I noticed the gross margin of Wheel Blue Bar in Gujarat. Exactly zero per cent.

From my experience, pricing never drives penetration or attracts new users. New users adopt a brand for three reasons: access, awareness and availability. The amount they consume has to do with their satisfaction with product quality and price. Lowering and increasing price changes consumption and not the recruitment of new users.

On a visit to a small village in rural Bihar eight years ago, I noticed that all the three shops in the village had stocked a small Rs 20 bar of Dove soap. I asked several women in the village whether they had used Dove soap. Yes, they told me. But occasionally, to wash their faces before they went for marriages.

Back in the office, I checked our household panel database and realized that 73 per cent of Dove users were low-income consumers, but they accounted for only half the volumes of the brand. The equity of the brand and the availability of the Rs 20 pack was making them occasional triers of the brand, but the high price was keeping them from consuming more. If we dropped the price on the brand, they would buy more but the moment we raised prices again they would go back to being occasional users.

Very rarely, price drops can cause volumes to fall. P. Govind Rajan was a sales manager when he saw that a drop in the price of Ponds Age Miracle resulted in dropped volumes as well. The price drop had taken the sheen off the aspiration quotient of the brand.

Equally, when a competitor drops price, you must immediately defend market share by dropping price no matter what the profit implication. D. Sundaram, former vice chairman and CFO, recalls how in 2004 when a competitor had dropped prices on detergents, HUL followed. He says he told analysts that the company is focused on long term and HUL will unblinkingly defend market shares. The share price indeed fell from Rs 250 to Rs 104, but thanks to this defence of this critical category, HUL has lived to see the day when its stock price has crossed Rs 2000.

Discounting in the hope of getting new users is such a common malaise that it is worth repeating why it doesn't work. Consumers decide to use a brand because they are persuaded or reminded of its benefits. If they are convinced, but can't afford it, they will buy it infrequently and that too a small pack of the product. Disrupting a category with a price drop is usually followed by the incumbent front runner also dropping the price, and it is then a race to the bottom. When prices are taken up again, users who entered through lower pricing exit with the same alacrity.

Those that build brands with the sword of discounted pricing tend to die by the sword of discounted pricing.

Price to What the Consumer Will Pay

Pricing is not a tool to recruit new users, it is a tool to maximize long-term value for shareholders. Long term is the key phrase. It is easy to price up in the short term even if one loses some volumes. But a loss in volumes has a long-term impact on profitability. Most companies either fix a profit margin they want to make and price accordingly or fix a price they believe the consumer is willing to pay and adjust the margin accordingly.

Neither is ideal since the former comes with the detriment of growth and the latter at the expense of margins. The HUL way is to figure out what consumers are willing to pay, have a margin in mind and work backwards at the costs. **The million-dollar question is of course determining what consumers are willing to pay.**

121

In the early 1990s the haircare team realized that to get shampoos to explode exponentially the price of the sachet had to be brought down from Rs 2 to Re 1. This would make no money for the company, but having first decided on the price, the team went about adjusting the cost base so they could make the target margins.

Harish Manwani, who was part of the team, recalls how the first step was better consumer understanding. Indian women have long hair and oil it once a week. They didn't need the conditioning that shampoos provided but they did need a better clean to get the oil out. The first step was removing expensive conditioning ingredients and replacing it with cheaper cleansers.

On the basis of the belief that volumes would grow exponentially, the company invested on large multi-track sachet packing machines ahead of demand. These increased capital costs but reduced production costs when scale was achieved. Third, the company lobbied hard with the government to reduce excise duties on shampoos from 120 per cent to eventually 30 per cent. The Re 1 sachet flew off the shelves and made money for HUL.

How do you decide to bring down prices from Rs 2 to Re 1? It is not a simple matter. The easiest way to assess what consumers are willing to pay for a product is to see what they are paying for similar products. HUL employs two tools to measure how competitive each brand is on pricing.

The Strategic Price Index (SPI) is an index set for the key product/pack combinations (also called SKU or stock keeping unit) compared to a key competitor. If Pepsodent 100 grams is supposed to operate at an SPI of 100 to a key competitor, and if the competitor moves the price from Rs 50 to Rs 52 then so does Pepsodent. SPI is a simple way to execute price changes, but the disadvantage is that it doesn't take into account the rest of the market. If the competitor takes bad pricing decisions, SPI will force HUL to take the same decision as well.

The second measure that HUL looks at is Relative Price Index (RPI), where the weighted average price per 100 grams for the entire category is assumed to be at RPI 100 and the RPIs of all products in the category are then calculated accordingly. Since RPI is the more fundamental measure and SPI the more convenient one, HUL brands first fix the RPI and then fix the SPI.

Airtel CEO Gopal Vittal believes that the secret sauce for HUL's long-term success is that in every category it operates it has a portfolio that straddles the price pyramid. This principle has helped HUL remain a bellwether company in times of boom when consumers typically upgrade to higher RPI brands or in slower times when they sometimes downgrade to lower-tier brands. The first principle of setting RPI is to have a portfolio of at least three brands at RPIs of roughly 80, 100 and 120.

Fixing an exact RPI for a brand is an un-exact task. One way to do it is to quantitatively model the RPI at which the brand was most successful. Let us say that over the last ten years the tea brand Taaza was most successful at an RPI of 82. Then the RPI is set at between 80 and 84. The biggest brand competing with Taaza is set as the benchmark for SPI.

If at the time Taaza was 82 RPI, its largest pack, Taaza 250 grams, was selling at a price premium of 20 per cent to Mohini tea, then the SPI of Taaza 250 grams is set as 120 to Mohini. The moment Mohini changes its price, a call from the sales force will tell the brand manager that the price of Taaza must change immediately as well. Of course a price drop by a competitor is often reported much faster than a price hike.

If Taaza's RPI is 82 and SPI 120 to Mohini, can this number ever change? There are two ways in which this can happen. If the equity of Taaza as measured by its equity score improves, it means that consumers may be willing to pay a slight premium for Taaza. In this case, HUL will experiment with a price hike of no more than 5 per cent above the SPI. If volumes continue to sustain at the same level, it means that the brand can perhaps afford to move to a higher SPI.

P. Govind Rajan tells a story about the time he was running HUL's profitable skincare category. One day he was called to his boss's room and asked why he had taken up the prices of Vaseline 100 ml. 'How do you know that I took up the prices?' asked Govind. 'My mother-in-law complained to me,' was his boss's answer. Govind replied that the fact that she continued to use it meant that his pricing decision was right. He showed his boss how six months before every price increase on Vaseline, advertising spends would go up, equity would get strengthened and the ground would be prepared for a price hike.

The second way in which SPI or RPI changes is if the business decides to make a change for a strategic reason. A few years ago, we realized that Taaza and Brooke Bond Red Label RPIs were too similar. We weren't straddling the price pyramid adequately and so we took a strategic call to drop the RPI. Money was taken out from packaging and tea flavour, an attribute that consumers didn't care much for. Strength and speed of infusion, crucial attributes for lower-income consumers, were left unchanged. As a consequence of this move, Taaza is now the most highly penetrated tea brand in India.

A third way to assess how much consumers are willing to pay for tea is to benchmark the price with the price of the underlying commodity of the brand. This overcomes the disadvantage of SPI (that it is linked to only one brand) and of RPI (that it is a slow and complex piece of data). Let us continue with the example of tea. If one has observed that tea sales are historically the best when the price HUL sells is at twice the price of the average tea auction price, then fix the price to raw material ratio as 1 to 2. As the auction price of tea moves up or down you can change the price of tea accordingly.

Using a combination of benchmark pricing and equity is an intuitive way to price in all categories. A few years ago we opened the Taj Mahal Tea House in Mumbai. It was housed in a heritage property, played classical music all day and had nooks and crannies where you could drink fine teas in solitude. This wasn't a business we knew well, and we wondered how to price our teas. Across the road was a Starbucks outlet and we decided to match their prices to begin with. A few months later we realized that we were getting a clientele that was older and wealthier and wanted to spend more time in our teahouse. So we took up prices by 20 per cent with no impact on sales. How pricing works in FMCG was exactly how it worked in hospitality.

Access Is More Important Than Affordability

As an area sales manager in Madhya Pradesh (MP) in 2000, I observed a funny difference in the behaviour of MP West and MP East. Whereas MP West consumers bought large packs of everything (Lifebuoy 600 grams and Surf 4 kilos), MP East consumers bought the smaller versions of the same brand (Lifebuoy 30 grams and Surf 200 grams). When I asked the old-timers the reason for this stark disparity, they said it was probably because MP East was a poorer tribal belt.

But an old lesson in business is never to believe an anecdote and so I looked up the per capita income of MP West and MP East. If one removed Bhopal and Indore, highly industrialized centres, from MP West, the incomes were exactly the same. But even the poorest areas of MP West, like Khandwa and Khargone in the Nimad belt, were buying large packs. More interestingly, while the pack sizes were different, the amount that consumers were buying was exactly the same every month. Lifebouy soap, I recall, was about 200 grams a month in both geographies. It is just that in MP West they were buying three months' stock in one shot, whereas in MP East they were buying five days' stock at a time.

The answer I realized after meeting a few farmers lay in rice and wheat. Rice, the staple of MP East, requires much more labour than wheat. Daily wage labour is employed in growing rice and salaries are paid daily. Shopping is done with much higher frequency and consumers demand smaller packs. Wheat and soya, the crops of MP West, are less labour-intensive and smallholder farmers grow it themselves.

Every six months when they harvest the crop, they get cash in hand and stock up for six months. Agriculture being the main employer in both geographies, this behaviour has a knockdown effect on people from other professions as well. To verify my theory, I looked at the sales data in Bhopal, a predominantly service-class city. Sure enough, Mrs Surma Bhopali was buying neither a very large pack nor a very small one. Like Goldilocks, she was buying a pack that was just right for a month's consumption – the 150 gram pack.

This insight around accessible price points being a more important factor than affordability, that is, price per kilo has made HUL famous across the world. The pioneering work done on shampoo sachets in the early 1980s opened up not just the shampoo category for HUL but also the premium detergent, skincare, toothpaste and coffee markets. On average most of these categories have 50 per cent of volume with sachets accounting for 80 per cent of users. Sachets have revolutionized the consumer goods industry in India.

There are some simple rules in managing a sachet business. The first and most important is that since it is about price points and not affordability, it is a cardinal mistake to have a cheaper product in the sachet compared to the large pack. Second, daily wage earning is much more common in rural India and so you need to have a distribution system in place. Third, consumers who want access to a category aren't usually the first ones to enter a category or brand. So don't launch access too early. Let the regular pack get to some sort of minimum penetration (say, 20 per cent) before launching access. Finally, pricing access packs is a skill and deserves a section for itself.

Discount Very Large Packs and Small Packs but by No More Than 20 Per Cent

Every product is available in several pack sizes or SKUs, as they are called in industry jargon. How does one price these SKUs? The simplest way of course is to calculate the price per kilo of the largest SKU and then price all SKUs at the same average price per kilo. So if the price of the 100 gram SKU of a product is Rs 10, then the 20 gram should be Rs 2 and the 1 kilo pack should be Rs 100. This misses two things: the first that the cost of production of different SKUs is different and second that the consumer for different packs is also different.

Let us take the larger pack sizes first. First, though it may well be the case, I haven't found enough evidence that selling a larger pack size makes consumers use more of a brand or that it prevents the competition from entering the pantry. But buyers of bigger pack sizes tend to be deal seekers and more importantly manufacturing big packs tends to cost less in terms of packaging and supply chain costs. So it is possible to pass on benefits to consumers who want a deal without company margins getting affected. As a rough rule, pass on all savings on big packs. As a rule of thumb this is around 10 per cent. The Brooke Bond Red Label 250 gram pack is priced at Rs 400 per kilo and the 1 kilo pack is priced at Rs 350.

Pricing small packs is one step more complex. Making small packs is actually more expensive than large packs – they reduce production capacity and use more packaging per kilo. Logically, the price per kilo of a small pack should be more than the price per kilo of a large pack. But the truth is that the consumers of small packs are generally much poorer than those of medium-size or large packs. So from a consumer point of view, it is better to discount the small packs, but ideally not by more than 15 to 20 per cent from the core pack. The worry that regular pack users will downgrade to sachets is usually unfounded. Shampoo sachets are significantly cheaper than bottles, but I suspect most readers of this book will still be bottle users. So the downgrading is limited. It is a case of robbing Peter to pay Paul, but since Peter is a lot richer it will make you feel like Robin Hood.

Pricing in Volatile Market Conditions

Over the past decade we have witnessed an unprecedented volatility of the prices of underlying commodities that constitute most household goods. Take the most influential of all commodities, crude oil. From 2000 to 2007 the price of crude oil broadly increased every year at a canter. But in 2008 it shot up from $90 to $160 a barrel and then dropped to $50 a barrel in 2009. It rose to $112 in 2012 before dropping to $36 in 2016 and then climbed back to its current levels of about $60 with many spikes and falls in between. There were sudden oil shocks in 1973, 1980, 1986 and 1998, but there has never been such a prolonged volatile period before. Pricing in times of volatile commodity prices is the new game in town for the last decade and calls for a different set of rules. Let me give an example where HUL got it horribly wrong.

Palm oil is the main feedstock in the manufacturing of toilet soaps. For a variety of reasons, palm oil prices are closely linked to crude oil prices. When, like crude oil, palm oil prices almost trebled between June 2006 and June 2008 HUL did two things: it took up prices at the same rate as costs and vacated the key price point packs of Rs 5 and Rs 10. Competition on the other hand took up prices much more slowly and cut advertising and promotions in this period. As a consequence, HUL lost market share, and since volumes in soaps matter a lot for profit margins (fixed costs are high), it lost margin as well. When palm oil prices were rising dizzyingly, HUL went long on palm oil and stocked up for several months. But between June 2008 and December 2009 palm oil prices fell from $1240 per tonne to $500 per tonne. Unfortunately, HUL was saddled with expensive stocks, and while the rest of the market dropped prices, HUL had to wait to finish its stock. When we dropped prices, we didn't pass on the entire cost benefit to the consumer, partly because we wanted structurally correct margins and partly because we were worried that the volume increase would not compensate the lower prices. When despite dropping prices volumes didn't come, HUL got desperate and passed on the entire cost drop to the consumer. Too late. Trade was stocked with higher price stocks (the original and the part price drop) and there was tremendous resistance to the last price. 'What do we do with the higher price stock?' was the refrain among shopkeepers. It took us a full year to get out of this mess.

There are several lessons from the pricing fiasco of soaps in the period 2007–10.

1.   When costs go up sharply, do not pass it on all at once to consumers. At some critical threshold (around a 10 per cent price hike), consumers start looking at other

brands. Once they start looking around, they will find another brand that suits them better.

2. Absorb the losses of a cost increase and cut non-essential costs in times of hyper-inflation.

3. Never vacate price point packs, whatever the provocation, without a proper long-term plan.

4. Don't overstock a commodity. In most businesses you are not likely to be an expert in predicting costs, like it happened with HUL with palm oil prices. Even if you do decide to stock up or down, do so by no more than for four weeks.

5. Don't get greedy and use a period of deflation to shore up your margins. You can only improve margins when your brand equity gets stronger.

6. When costs fall, drop prices in one shot, reflecting the entire cost drop. Sequential price drops lead to choked pipelines.

HUL has learnt from its mistakes of 2008 and 2009 and is now a master of pricing in volatile conditions.

In the next chapter we will learn about HUL's mighty sales system, but first, a summary of this chapter.

Summary

1. Price discounts do not recruit new consumers; they merely get existing consumers to buy a bit more.
2. Fix the price the consumer will pay, the margin you want and then get the right costs.
3. Assess the price consumers are willing to pay to benchmark yourself versus competitors, the market or the underlying commodity.
4. Build a portfolio of brands at different price points to be resilient in times of crises.
5. Lower price point is more important than cheaper price per kilo for low-income consumers.
6. Price different pack sizes differently depending on consumer profile and cost structure.
7. Pricing under volatile conditions requires special rules.

6

Why Sales Is Not a Revenue Function

Sales Management Lessons from Hindustan Unilever

Sales Is a Cost Centre, Not a Revenue Centre

Our sales director Srinandan 'Tan' Sundaram gave me this brilliant insight: 'Sales is a cost centre and not a revenue centre. Once you are clear on this, everything else about managing a sales and distribution system is easy.' What Tan was saying was that brands and not the sales function generate sales. The job of a sales system is to fulfil demand in the lowest-cost possible. Pipes don't quench thirst, water does. Roads don't take you to a destination, your desire to go does. Roads and pipes, like the sales system, are mere enablers.

This is a controversial point and till I spoke to Tan I myself was not sure of this. Sales is a central role in every organization and especially so in HUL. Directly covering 1.5 million outlets every week, the HUL sales system is legendary across the world for its might. It covers villages not reached by any other company and sometimes even the government. Some may think it is the core competence of HUL. It is not. It is a competitive advantage, but HUL's core competence is in building brands and nurturing people.

There are several examples where HUL's distribution power has come a cropper when the brand thinking hasn't been right. A few years ago, we launched a Knorr range of blended masalas like pav bhaji masala and chole masala. The products were good but masalas is a solved problem in India, with several brands operating in blended spices. Despite a massive distribution drive, the project failed. Trying to meet an already met need with better distribution does not work. The opposite does not hold true, though. Every category we have built, be it Wheel in the 1980s or Vim in the 1990s or hair conditioners a decade ago or green tea and Indulekha more recently, would not have been created without sales being an enabler. With more time and more money, most companies may have got the same result. But the HUL system gives speed and low costs – both massive competitive advantages.

Sales is a cost centre and not a revenue centre is a *contradiction obvious in hindsight.* Brilliant insights can come from everywhere, not just from marketing.

Be Available but Never in Too Much Quantity

In 2001 HUL, then HLL, relaunched the sales system using a new method called the HLL way. The core premise of the HLL way was that sales can benefit the business by ensuring availability, visibility and dealer recommendation. Availability simply means making the product available in as many stores as possible. I hope my publishers make this book available in as many retail bookstores as possible.

Visibility means displaying posters of the product or making it prominently visible on the shelf. HUL believes that this is essentially a marketing and not sales task and has a separate merchandising force doing this. Visibility is a marketing task sometimes done conveniently by the sales team.

Dealer recommendation means that the dealer goes out of his way to recommend a product to a customer. It is believed that dealers recommend a product either because it is profitable or because they have so much of it in their store that they want to reduce their stock. Dealer recommendation was the conceptual argument to justify depth selling into an outlet – selling much more than required to push for value sales.

A few years ago Mickey Sharma, the ice cream sales head of our South branch, and I visited a small store in a suburb of Chennai. It was a blazing May and peak season for ice creams. The Kwality Wall's cabinet was packed with every single product we had. I was about to compliment the salesperson for a great job done when a little girl walked in and asked for a Rs 10 Orange Ice Lolly. The shopkeeper went to the cabinet and gave her a competition ice lolly. I glowered at the salesperson. Had he forgotten to sell our fastest-selling product? The shopkeeper came to his rescue instantly. When the salesperson filled the cabinet two days ago, he had indeed sold ice lolly. But it had run out.

What happened dawned on me when I looked at his last bill from us. The shopkeeper sold Rs 10,000 worth of ice cream every month, and two days ago the salesperson had sold him Rs 5000 worth of stock. This was a composite of low-priced, fast-moving stock like the lolly and expensive products like Magnum. The ice lolly, the fastest-moving product, had sold out in a day, but since the retailer owed HUL Rs 5000, or two weeks' sales, he didn't have the money to pay up in two days.

A second order must have been rejected because the first bill hadn't been paid, and to prevent consumers like the little girl from going away the shopkeeper had paid Rs 500 in cash and bought orange lolly from a competitor. Our salesperson visited the outlet twice a week, and if instead of selling Rs 5000 worth of stocks once and nothing for the next three visits, he had sold Rs 1250 worth of stocks on each of the four visits, we wouldn't have lost the little girl who asked for an ice lolly.

There are two lessons here. One, for salespeople, who should sell just what is adequate till their next visit. Second, for marketing people, the more the products you launch and insist that they find their place on the shelf, the more retailer capital you block and the more likely it is that your core products will go out of stock. I have covered the problem of excess brand extensions in chapter two, but here is a real example.

Physical availability or distribution is the raison d'être for a sales system. The more outlets you are available in (in the right quantity), the more the sales. Rohit Jawa, currently chairman of Unilever China, recalls his days as a young sales manager in Rajasthan in the early 1990s. He realized that in a geographically big state like Rajasthan, the moment he reduced the distance between a distributor and an outlet, sales would go up. He bought a census of Rajasthan and painstakingly mapped all towns where we could viably appoint a distributor. He grew his distributors from 100 to 168 and his sales grew from 12–13 per cent to 30 per cent. This bears out a general rule in distribution that a former boss told me: for every 10 per cent growth in distribution, expect a 3.5 per cent increase in sales.

Like marketing activities should focus on getting users

and not worry about consumption, sales managers should focus on availability and frequency of bills being generated and not depth of sales.

Focus on How Fast Your Product Sells, Not on the Margin

Professor M.N. Vora was a legendary professor at IIMA who taught us sales management. He had a trick question for us once. Would you rather be a roadside seller of T-shirts who sold his stock every day but made only 1 per cent margin or the owner of a fancy high street store who made 30 per cent margin on clothes but sold the stock once every three months. He would answer his own question by saying that the humble roadside seller rotates (the number of times you sell paid-up stock) his stock 365 times a year and makes 365 per cent return on his stock while the high street store owner who rotates his stock four times a year makes only 120 per cent return on his stock. A no-brainer: rotation not margin is king in business.

Calculating distributor return on investment (RoI) is the very first task HUL management trainees are taught. You calculate the sales for the year and multiply it by margins to arrive at his net revenue. Next you subtract his costs – salespeople, petrol, discounts, and depreciation on his fixed costs like vehicles and computers – to arrive at his net profit. You then divide this by his investment in stock and credit to get the RoI. So if a distributor had a margin of 5 per cent, costs of 3 per cent, held two weeks of stocks and two weeks of his credit was locked in the market, his RoI was 24 per cent. Subtract the costs from the margin and multiply it by the number of rotations (in this case the rotations are twelve since he holds a month of stocks plus credit). We would have endless debates with the distributor on the fine points of accounting. Do we account for his effort in salaries, what happens if he owns the godown himself, etc., but broadly the entire HUL partner system is aligned to measuring RoI.

Once you move the conversation to RoI and not margins, it can be a win–win for both the company and its distributors. Suppose we cut the margin by 1 per cent and reduced the stocks to three days and the credit in the market to seven days. The investment reduces to ten days and on a reduced net margin of 1 per cent the retailer gets 35 rotations or an RoI of 35 per cent. HUL saves 1 per cent and the distributor RoI actually goes up. At the heart of how HUL works in sales lies a ruthless focus on reducing working capital and getting the commensurate benefit in terms of margins.

In 2012 I spent half a day sitting at the biggest wholesaler's (a wholesaler sells to smaller shops and not to end consumers) outlet in Wardha (famous for its Gandhi ashram) near Nagpur. I was observing how small retailers interact with the wholesaler. I must have seen about a hundred small shopkeepers buy from the wholesaler and I observed three things.

None of them asked about the margin, the wholesaler recommended no product to them and they asked only for the fastest-selling SKUs. The pink version of Lux soap, not the blue version. A godown check of the tiny shop (despite having huge sales) revealed one day of stock of only the core SKUs. So the retailers were not shopping for high-margin products but for high-velocity products. The wholesalers were not selling high-margin products and were only stocking high-rotation products. **Velocity always trumps margins.**

P. Govind Rajan recalls a time as brand manager on Wheel when he realized that while Nirma sold twice the volumes of Wheel detergent, both of them were sold in bags weighing 50 kilos to a retailer. Understanding that with half the velocity the retailer would make half the RoI on a bag of the same size, Govind reduced the bag size to 25 kilos. Now both brands made the same RoI to a retailer and distribution of Wheel soared.

Early in my career as a sales manager I firmly believed that sales can make a real difference to, well, 'sales'. I ran innovative wholesale schemes, charged the team to do big sales numbers in one day and rewarded the guys who delivered the best sales that month. The short-term results were good, but they would make no difference a few months down the line.

By and by I realized that investment in infrastructure that drove more coverage was the key to success. But distributors would never agree to infrastructure investments until their RoI improved. Changing margin was non-negotiable, so I did two things.

I realized that up to two days of stocks that were sitting in the godowns were slow-moving stocks – innovations that didn't fire, stock that only sold in season, etc. I got a special budget for slow-moving stocks and liquidated it. One reason that distributors carried two weeks of stock was that they received a shipment only once a week. Along with buffers and slow-moving stock, a weekly delivery meant a minimum of two weeks of stocks. But a biweekly delivery meant that there wouldn't be enough load for trucks to go full. Distribution costs would go up.

Using my good offices with the depot and supply chain, I convinced them that if they clubbed three to four drop points with every truckload, I would reduce the overall stocks not just at the distributor but also at the depot (a key objective of depot managers). Reducing slow-moving stocks and increasing delivery frequency increased the investment the distributor was able to put into infrastructure. The growth we now saw was sustainable.

That rotation is important does not mean that margins have no role in ensuring availability. Swarnim Bharadwaj, a former brand manager on Lux, says, 'In the soaps category we figured out that discounts to wholesalers were simply increasing stock in their storerooms but not having any effect on consumer offtake and so we slowly whittled down all trade schemes to zero. In most cases there was a short blip in sales as stocks adjusted but consumer offtake was unaffected, and we redeployed the money to other more productive uses.

'However, on Lux and Lifebuoy Rs 10 bars [the mainstay of HUL's business in North India] sales started falling and on a visit to rural UP I discovered why. For the longest time, wholesalers had purchased a dozen bars from HUL at Rs 105 and sold them by the dozen to small retailers at Rs 110, thereby making a profit of Rs 5. The small retailers would in turn sell each bar for Rs 10 [a total of Rs 120] and make a profit of Rs 10 on a dozen. When we removed the trade schemes the price to wholesalers went from Rs 105 a dozen to Rs 109 a dozen. Normally this would have prompted the wholesaler to increase his selling price from Rs 110 to Rs 112 or Rs 113 to protect his profit but in this case the selling price of Rs 110 a dozen to small retailers had become an established

trade price point and wholesalers were unable to move it up. Hence their profits tanked and so did their interest in selling HUL bars. On discovering this we promptly restored the incentives and sales came right back. We had long known the concept of consumer price points such as Rs 5 or Rs 10, but trade price points were a new thing we discovered with this experience.'

The next time you are in a shop, any shop, look around you. Is it one where you see a few fast-selling products in every category (*sui se leke haathi*, from needles to elephants, as my former sales officer Uttam Patil was fond of saying) or one where you see a wide range of slow movers in a few categories? You may be lulled into thinking that it is better to shop in the latter. Not so. The former shop will be doing better not only financially but also in terms of ease of search, service and even discounts on products you really want. And chances are in the former you will find what you are looking for, but in the latter, it will be out of stock. **Range reduces the availability of what you really want to buy.**

Measure Input Not Output of a Sales System

Sales, along with supply chain, is the most measurable function in an organization. It is easy to measure the costs of a factory and its productivity just as it is easy to measure the sales a salesperson makes. So should salespeople be rewarded on the sales they generate?

Rewarding a salesperson for sales is an easy solution, but it is like rewarding a road contractor for the number of cars that travel on the road. If one takes Tan's principle to the logical conclusion – that sales is not a revenue function – **then sales teams shouldn't be rewarded for bringing in revenue; instead they should be rewarded for creating the enablers of revenue.**

When Sanjay Dube became head of the HUL sales system in 2005, he made some radical changes to salespeople bonuses. Only a fraction of the reward was linked to sales and the bulk of the reward was linked to whether a salesperson made a bill, however small, at a store and whether visibility of our brands in terms of posters, shelf display, etc., was in place. But measuring visibility is tough, so Sanjay set up a detective system that would randomly audit stores every month and give a visibility execution score to each salesperson.

Krishnan Sundaram, currently a vice president at HUL in charge of the GSK integration, has written a paper on the history of HUL's tea business. He writes that Brooke Bond salespeople were incentivized on the volume of tea sold, and hence depots linked to wholesale markets were coveted as they meant better pay and often easier work. As a consequence, the Brooke Bond operation had significant leakages and was also very inward-focused. This lack of customer and consumer focus as well as the tendency of well-entrenched front-line salespeople to favour a few meant that when Brooke Bond faced tough competition, they lost market shares rather quickly.

DMart, India's most valuable retailer, has several HUL alumni, including its CEO, Neville Noronha, running it. DMart store managers don't have a sales target for their store; instead they have a target for on-shelf availability and pilferage. These are the only input variables they control. According to a BloombergQuint report in 2017, on key measures like profit per square foot DMart outperforms its competitors 4:1.

So why do so many companies reward output and not input? For one, many believe that sales systems generate revenue, but the other real problem is that input metrics can easily be fudged. When I joined the HUL sales system, my predecessor warned me of the bubble gum theory of distribution. Every salesperson would show more and more shops being directly visited (remember there are 12 million stores in India and even after all these years HUL only visits 1.8 million).

The moment he left his successor would burst the bubble and show that 30 per cent of the outlets were either false or were just not economical to cover. He would reduce the outlets under his supervision, only to blow his own bubble for a few years. Forget about measuring coverage. Instead, focus on sales, he sagely told me. If sales happen, it means more outlets are being covered.

But as I realized, this is not true. Sales can happen if you stuff your distributors and retailers with stock or if you undercut the rate so that a wholesaler in your geography throws stock in another one. I was caught between the devil of not being able to measure distribution and the deep sea of not knowing whether sales were happening in the right way.

But in today's digital age that is not an excuse. Every input metric can be measured most efficiently: salespeople book orders on apps in their phones which can track what time they started work and whether they visited every shop they claim to have. If you want to confirm that they have stuck a poster in a shop, ask them to take a photo of the poster and you can ensure it is the right geotagged outlet.

All of us in any business we run must ensure that at least 75 per cent of rewards is input- and not output-linked.

The Right Behaviours in a Sales Team

There is a stereotype of the ideal salesperson: an aggressive go-getter with a can-do spirit. One who drinks late into the night and wakes up early in the morning to go back to the market to make sales calls. He delivers his numbers month after month, and young trainee salespeople model themselves on him.

Tan, our sales director, believes that this is a dangerous stereotype that encourages individual glory-seeking, which he identifies as the root cause for the destruction of a sales system. Seeking to be the fastest growing in sales inevitably means higher stocks in trade, less focus on rotation and increased selective margins, which cause trade price instability. This takes away investments from things that can actually build the roads and pipes that help brands grow.

Tan remembers that when he was an ASM a competition was run on Clinic Plus sachets measured by which area in the company would sell the most. Competition among the already competitive ASMs was high, and record sales were hit. Unfortunately, the next two months saw very poor sales and in three months they were back to square one.

But if not on sales targets achieved, how does one keep a sales system passionate? After all, it is a routine job that requires energy that sales targets provide. Tan says a few key inputs must be identified and passion for these inputs must be created. These inputs could be new stores added, bills made and execution of new launches. A few years ago, I moved the targets of ice cream salespeople from only sales to bills made in an outlet. There were loud protests, and salespeople would start making smaller bills on each visit so that they could make more bills. That is what happened, but as a consequence slow-moving stock which would prevent the next bill from being made was no longer sold and overall sales went up. By giving a non-sales metric (bills cut) to a salesperson, we saw sales move up.

Apart from discouraging glory-seeking behaviour, Tan believes that sales systems should be rooted in fact and not anecdote. Anecdotes, he says, give far too much weightage to the peaks of a sales system. Working till midnight to finish a daily target makes for a great anecdote, but it conveniently forgets to mention what happens the day after. While anecdotes may add spice to the daily life in sales, the meat and potatoes of the sales system must be anchored in fact.

Sanjay Dube says that in sales more than in any other function, integrity of the leader is paramount. This is because salespeople do not work in a supervised environment. The way of working is left to the individual's value system. Hence leading by example and consistently demonstrating the right way is required of the leadership.

Hemant Bakshi, a former director at HUL, recalls the 'two-wallet' rule his boss, a sales officer called Kalsi, gave him when he was a management trainee. The rule was that anything spent for the company had to be separate from personal spending. In those days, employees were given cash advances, which they would then settle with the company by submitting an expense statement. Two wallets were required, one for personal spending and one for company spending. Not only that, the second wallet had at all times to contain the exact amount of the advance less the amount submitted in the expense statements. The company wallet would be randomly checked and if the amount was less than what it should be the person would be summarily dismissed.

My early sales stint has been my most memorable job in HUL. I was a twenty-three-year-old, a Mumbaiwallah who had just got his MBA from IIMA. Not the right kind of background that prepares you for leading large numbers of people, several old enough to be your father, in wild Madhya Pradesh. But over time they became my second family.

Fifteen years after I left MP we had a reunion of my sales force near Alibaug, a beach resort near Mumbai. Most of us showed up grey-haired, with receding hairlines and pot bellies. The party went on late into the night with all of us recounting our favourite stories. Our paths in these fifteen years had been very different, but all of us felt a moment of connection when we met again. That in the final reckoning is the real joy of working for HUL, and to me earning the love and respect of my sales force twenty years ago in MP remains the achievement I am most proud of.

Summary

If you think the sales system is a revenue generator you focus on sales pressure, trade margins and glory-seeking behaviour and ultimately cut the investments required for a good sales system. The moment you think of it as a cost centre you focus on availability, keeping stocks low, rotating key products faster and a culture that is based on facts: 100 out of 100 times the latter will win.

1. Sales is a cost and not a revenue centre.
2. Focus on availability of products and not on depth of stock.
3. Don't hold high stocks in the system and give excessive margins. Instead keep stocks low and ensure rotation.
4. Drive the sales system on input metrics rather than output metrics, but ensure input metrics are measured robustly and can't be fudged.
5. Cut glory-seeking behaviour in your sales teams.
6. Build a fact-based and not an anecdote-based culture.

7

Respect for Money

Cost Management Lessons from Hindustan Unilever

As Long as Costs Exist, Savings Are Possible

The annual chairman's conference is a sombre affair at HUL. During my management training stint, a tutor warned me to dress decently and arrive on time. 'I don't care whether you are noticed, but frankly if you are noticed I will be noticed,' he told me ominously. I took serious note and arrived in sparkling formals a full thirty seconds before our chairman Vindi Banga went on stage. Vindi reviewed the performance of the business and of each category. When he came to costs, he said that in his experience HUL was like a large fruit-laden tree. Even after plucking every single fruit, when you shake it, more fruit falls. And if you shake it again, even more fruit falls. Cost management at HUL is like the famous Akshay Patra that yields untold bounties, endlessly.

There are many ways to assess how cost efficient a company is. Two simple metrics are employee cost and return on capital employed. Employee cost as a percentage of turnover shows how much productive value a company gets from its people. ROCE measures show how much value a company extracts from its capital. If you have bought a house for Rs 1 crore and you get an annual rent of Rs 4 lakh from it, your ROCE is 4 per cent.

Let us see how HUL compares with its peers in the consumer goods space. Its employee cost is 4 per cent of its turnover compared to a benchmark of 7 per cent and its ROCE is 92 per cent compared to 33 per cent for the industry. These are not just best in class numbers within consumer goods, but best in class across industries.

Year Ended March 2019	HUL	Dabur	GCPL	Marico	Nestlé	ITC	Peer group
Sales (Rs crore)	38,400	6,200	5,800	5,900	11,200	45,000	74,000
Employee cost (%)	4	9	6	5	10	6	7
ROCE (%)	92	38	31	34	41	31	33

Source: www.moneycontrol.com

What makes HUL such a good cost manager? D. Sundaram says change is continuous and causes obsolescence of certain processes. But if one is not vigilant of this the costs associated with those processes can continue. As long as there is change, there will always be hidden costs and one needs to scrutinize such processes and costs. Cost reduction, he says, is never a 'cul de sac nor a dead end'. There is always more to do.

Harish Manwani had the ability to synthesize complex thoughts in pithy one-liners. One of his favourites was 'Fix the price and the profit you want to make; the cost is the target you have to achieve.' It is a disruptive thought. Most companies assume the costs and then fix one of the other two – price or profits. Multinationals tend to fix the profit they want and price accordingly, and local competitors fix a price and take a reduction on profits. HUL alone, in my knowledge, fixes profit and price and treats cost as a variable.

I recently saw a faded price board of Kwality Wall's Ice Cream from 2004. The evergreen vanilla cup was Rs 10 on the price board, just as it is today fifteen years later. HUL has played every trick in the book to ensure that this price point is not violated: from reducing grammage per cup to better supply chain efficiencies to technologies like fat homogenization to reduce the vacant airspace in a vanilla ice cream cup. A great example of the principle 'price for the consumer, fix the profit and then work away at the costs'.

The most important reason Harish's formula works is that price is the biggest driver of volumes and volumes are the biggest driver of cost reduction. By fixing prices low, you drive volumes up and costs down.

Why do volumes drive costs down?

All costs are either variable, like raw materials and

power, or fixed, like rent, advertising, salaries of office staff, etc. If the fixed costs are 20 per cent of revenue and revenue doubles, the fixed costs come down to 10 per cent of revenue. This is called leverage, where costs come down not because you cut it, but because the business becomes bigger. More interestingly, even those that are considered variable costs are not fully variable and have large fixed components to them. Take raw material costs, clearly a variable cost. But the more volume you produce, the less the wastage in factories and the better your negotiation power. The more the volumes, the less the chances of trucks going half full or energy being wasted in factory shutdowns. So in reality you get leverage not just on fixed costs but even on what are considered variable costs.

Now that we have understood that growth is the biggest driver of cost reduction, let us understand how to reduce actual costs. There are four big elements of cost in any P&L statement. The cost of materials, the cost of supply chain, which includes making and distributing, the cost of advertising and the indirect or overhead costs, which include salaries and other administrative expenses. Let us look at how HUL works at reducing each of these.

Samir Jain, currently CEO of Bungee, was the chief packaging buyer at HUL when he realized two things. Every factory was buying cardboard boxes (CLD, in HUL jargon) from three or four suppliers. Supply security was the reason. Samir realized that having several suppliers makes you less important to each supplier, thereby affecting supply security. It is the chicken-and-egg story. The more you push for supply security by fragmenting supplier base, the less likely you are to achieve it. Instead, if you become crucial to the business of a single supplier, you not only reduce costs but also ensure that it will do its best to ensure supplier security. Each region was given one supplier to work with, with a supplier from another region as the backup. Costs went down and supply security did indeed go up.

Materials: Design for Output and Not Input

Most consumers want benefits from products at the cheapest cost. A vocal few, usually higher income, demand specific ingredients. There is no value judgement here and companies should service the needs of their consumers in the best way. HUL being a predominantly mass marketing company, it usually designs for output and not input.

Categories can often get locked into high-priced raw materials if their formulations are input- and not output-focused. Imagine a master chef who has a recipe for his secret masala: it contains turmeric from Meghalaya, chillies fresh from Mexico, coarse sea salt and saffron from Spain. Tastes wonderful but costs the earth, especially when the rupee depreciates versus the euro. There is another approach to deconstructing this masala: it has a certain shade of yellow that is measurable, aromas that can be measured on an olfactometer, a certain combination of the five basic tastes of salt, sweet, sour, umami and bitter, a certain average particle size and a certain nutrition profile. Once you know these parameters you can formulate for these output variables. Turmeric from Greece can be replaced by Salem turmeric and you could add deflavoured mango powder to get the same shade of yellow. The possibilities are endless, creative and cheaper. To hell with the food snobs.

Consider the debate on ice cream versus frozen foods. Ice cream in most countries is defined in a way that is neutral to the type of fat used, milk or vegetable. In India regulation states that ice cream can only be called so if it is made from milk fat; if it is made from vegetable fat, it is called frozen dessert. HUL makes both, because it understands each gives a different benefit. Milk fat has a distinctive milky note which people in the northern and western parts of the country prefer. Vegetable fat is cheaper, carries flavour better, is on balance healthier (less cholesterol and saturated fat) and is preferred in the eastern and southern parts of the country. The important thing is that HUL designs for benefits that consumers seek and not ingredients that consumers do not really care about.

The oil buying process is another example of output-focused design. Soap, which is primarily made from oil, must lather but it also needs a certain hardness in structure. Coconut oil gives great lather but is very soft. PFAD, a fractionate of palm oil, is hard but doesn't lather as well. Palm kernel oil (PKO) does both moderately. A soap formulation could be 20 per cent coconut oil, 30 per cent palm kernel and 50 per cent PFAD.

But what does one do when coconut prices shoot through the roof? Can you replace it with some PKO and compensate for the reduced softness by also reducing PFAD? The HUL way is to specify certain lather and hardness value for the soap and continuously change formulations so that the cheapest formulation at any given time that meets both criteria is in the market.

Another principle in designing for output is to **spend money only on things consumers are willing to pay for.**

P. Govind Rajan, currently CEO of Cuemath, an edtech start-up, gives a great example in personal care. A big cost in packaging of bottles is the one-time cost of the mould required to shape a bottle. Interestingly, the cost of the mould of a cap is four to five times that of a mould of a bottle. So HUL ensures that even though we have different shapes and sizes of bottles, the caps of all these are the same. It is a small idea, but has a dramatic impact on costs.

There is a lot of raw material that gets wasted that consumers often find value in. Certain parts of plucked tea (the stems and large leaves) contain very little 'teaness' (a combination of caffeine, polyphenols and volatile flavours) and look very different from the rest of the tea leaf. Most tea manufacturers throw this away as fodder. But they do contain some 'tea'. So HUL devised a way to make them into small pellets and mix these with very good quality tea to get an average quality tea that had some consumer value.

Designing for output that consumers value and not for input is one of the key differentiating factors of a company that is great on costs.

A Lean Supply Chain

A lean supply chain does three things: it extracts more from fixed capital, creatively reduces operating costs and sells close to the factory.

Extract more from fixed capital

Many people believe that while fixed cost leverage works up to a certain point, volume growth beyond that point always requires new fixed costs. The idea of pricing to drive leverage doesn't appeal to them since they believe that life catches up with them in the next round of capital expansion. They work on the principle that all costs are fixed. The belief at HUL on the other hand is that all costs are variable. If you grow beyond the capacity of a factory, you'll need a new one, more overheads, etc. It is like the common woe in the airline industry on filling seats in empty planes. If you cut prices, seats do fill up and very soon you need new aircraft that again need filling up. You are now left with unfilled seats at lower prices!

HUL is a master of extracting more from fixed capital. Every manufacturing process is thoroughly studied and de-bottlenecked to increase rated capacity. Pradeep Banerjee, executive director supply chain and a company veteran of forty years, has a 50:25:25 rule when it comes to capital expenses: 50 per cent of new capacity must come from de-bottlenecking, 25 per cent from efficiencies like factory worker productivity and only 25 per cent from new capital.

He gave me the example of the soap drying process. Every time volumes went up, the factory had to order a new dryer. Increasing the temperature in the dryer to dry the soap quickly was not possible because this created extra water vapour, which again wet the soap. A smart engineer designed a downstream solution for dealing with the vapour and suddenly the capacity of the same machine doubled.

This obsession with low capital spends is why HUL's ROCE, at 93 per cent, is the highest in the industry.

Arun Adhikari, a former managing director at HUL, believes that 'respect for money' is a key value system in HUL and it is best evinced by its attitude to capital expenditure. He recalls a story of when his friend Durgesh Mehta was the branch accountant at the Calcutta branch. Durgesh wanted a Godrej Storewell cupboard in his room and made a capital expenditure proposal citing security of crucial financial documents as the reason. The reply from the capex approval authority was that the proposal had been partly approved. The request for the cupboard was disallowed but an upgrade of the existing lock to the door to his room was approved. A more secure lock to the room would surely solve the problem of theft of important documents!

Arun also recalls a meeting where the factory manager of one of HUL's factories raised a request for a new badminton net. The chairman of the company who was present at the meeting asked how many holes there were in the net. When told there were three, he said that surely that didn't deserve a new net and some darning would do.

Apart from fixed capital, HUL's obsession with working capital is legendary. Working capital includes credit and stocks in hand and it is famously (though not accurately) said in corporate circles that HUL operates with negative working capital. When Rohit Jawa was training in Shahjahanpur, near Bareilly, he recalls, he got information that a distributor's cheque had bounced. This meant unpaid company working capital was lying with the distributor. Jawa finished his dinner and rode his bike through dacoit-infested areas to the distributor's house. Knocking on the door at 10 p.m., he demanded and got the cash back.

Reducing operating costs

Reducing operating factory costs such as energy, secondary packing material, labour cost, etc., requires both creativity and often courage.

Our supply chain director, Pradeep Banerjee, who co-authored this chapter with me, narrated an example of the time he was a young technical manager fresh out of IIT-Delhi. Glycerine, a valuable by-product of the soap-making process, has to be extracted by evaporating it from a dilute water solution. It is an energy-intensive process. Pradeep realized that the best way to evaporate something faster is by agitating it with hot steam. It was a common enough process, except that here you were adding water in the form of steam to remove water from glycerine. In many places the idea would have been shot down, but HUL, with its penchant for creative cost solutions, invested in the equipment and achieved outstanding results.

The speed of a sachet packing line is determined by the number of sachets it produces per 'stroke'. If the sachets are designed horizontally you may get five, but if designed vertically you get ten sachets per stroke. The more vertical the design the less visible it is on the shelf, but the better the production efficiency. So HUL designed a jodi pack, two strips of relatively thin sachets, loosely attached together to get the right size and good shelf visibility.

Apart from creativity, reducing structural costs often needs a lot of courage. Keki Dadiseth, a former chairman, recalls how HUL managed its Mumbai factory lockout in 1988. The Mumbai factory then accounted for 60 per cent of HUL's production, but finding the demands of the unions increasingly unreasonable, the management decided not to give in further and to lock out the factory instead of accepting an indefinitely increasing cost base.

Preparations for this eventuality had begun in 1986. In those days, capacities were licensed and could not be easily added, but HUL cleverly used an exemption on this rule for 100 per cent subsidiaries to set up capacity in backward sites in the name of its subsidiaries. Companies weren't allowed to use contract manufacturers, but if you leased their sites you could let them run the factory.

Finally, HUL rapidly moved equipment to existing factories in sites like Khamgaon and Yavatmal using decongestion of Mumbai as an excuse. Thus, not only was HUL able to withstand the strike for almost ten months, but when the strike ended its manufacturing costs had come down significantly.

Distribution: Produce close to the market or the raw material source

Transportation of goods and services adds no value to the consumer experience, and you can always save money here. The key principle in distribution cost management is to produce close to either the market or the source of the raw material.

As a general manager of our soaps business, I would regularly visit our factory in Orai near Lucknow. The factory was operating at 50 per cent of its capacity. There is nothing as dispiriting as seeing machinery and workers idle. Over tender kakori kababs with the factory manager, K.C. Katoch, we tried to find a solution.

It turned out that three-fourths of the factory costs that were allocated to the Lux bar were fixed. An underutilized factory meant much higher costs. If we sold only in the shadow of the factory, instead of sending soap all over the country, we could distribute it at a fraction of the cost.

The savings from distribution and better utilization of the factory could be used to fund a big price drop.

What if we made a special Lux pack only to be sold in central UP, a geography as large as France in population, at a much lower price than the national price. We overrode several objections and quickly implemented the plan. In no time Orai was back to being a humming factory.

P. Govind Rajan, who was brand manager on Wheel detergent, recalls that while competing with Nirma prices were fixed and product quality was also fixed. To make margins HUL had to really think out of the box. They realized that the cost component in Wheel was in transporting salt (yes, cheaper detergents use salt as a filler) across the country. So they set up a large Wheel factory right next to the salt mines in Gujarat with a pipe directly going from the mines to the factory.

Advertising: Pay for Media Reach, Cut the Other Costs

Talking about his two employers, R. Gopalakrishnan said that there was a simple difference between Lever and Tata. While Tata was very liberal with spending capital, every rupee of advertising had to be accounted for. HUL, on the other hand, was liberal with advertising but extremely careful in capital spending.

But despite being liberal in advertising spending, HUL is careful to categorize good and bad cost in advertising. The general principle here is that deployed media is good because consumers see the brand, but the cost of producing ads needs to be carefully monitored.

We have already discussed why spending your money on one ad is better in terms of reach than spending the money on four or five ads. It is even better on costs because ad production costs are saved. An ad can run for much longer periods than most people think, and it is a common cliché at HUL that brand managers get bored of the ad before consumers.

My former boss Sandeep Kataria once told me about an ad his predecessor Vivek Rampal had made on the brand Rin. It was a pretty average ad, but Vivek ran it for three years till every consumer remembered it. The salience driven by consistency (not great advertising) not only made a difference to sales but also cut advertising production costs.

The one area where advertising production cannot count the pennies is in getting high quality creative people working on the brand. We will talk about that in the next section.

Why Paying More Saves Cost: The War on Overheads

In March 2018 an *Economic Times* article said that among Indian companies HUL had the largest number of people earning more than Rs 1 crore a year. In its most recent annual report, HUL declared 143 people earning over Rs 1 crore. This is about 10 per cent of the management force, which almost certainly is at the top end of the industry. How does this statistic of highly paid executives reconcile with the fact that at 4 per cent, HUL's employee costs are the lowest in the industry?

Sanjeev Mehta's mantra for people costs is 'pay six people the salary of eight people and get them to do the job of ten people', implying pay well but drive productivity even harder. There are several ways HUL does this. It recruits the best people from campuses, gives them big responsibilities early and most importantly rates them as far as possible on output rather than input metrics.

Revenue is a better target to give a marketing person than quality of advertising, which is a better measure to give than number of new campaigns in the year. Margins are a better target to give a supply chain person rather than overall factory costs, which is better than salary of labour in the factory. Being output-focused channels efforts in the desired direction, makes resources flexible and everyone in the system cost-conscious. The exception to this rule of output targets is in the sales force, where input target ensures better discipline. But everywhere else try to set output targets.

Apart from salaries there are plenty of other overheads: office rentals, transport costs, conference costs, communication, etc. In all these areas, D. Sundaram emphasizes the principle that since these costs are not revenue-facing and only affect convenience of employees, they should be kept to the minimum required for basic comfort. Higher-paid employees who have to rough it out at work are better motivated than lower-paid employees who have luxurious facilities. HUL guest houses are clean and well kept, but without the trappings of fancy hotels, from tube lights to blankets that just about cover the toes of a six-footer like myself.

Apart from salaries, there is another area where HUL often pays more to save cost. Samir Jain recalls how there was an unwritten code of honour that if a supplier came up with an innovation that saved costs to the company, the company would persist with him for a long time even if there were cheaper options available. He remembers how changing from paper to a polylaminate in soap packaging was a saving and increased productivity. The supplier who came up with the idea continued to be the sole supplier of this laminate even when it had become industry standard.

Summary

1. Volumes are the biggest driver of costs.
2. Design for output and not input.
3. Keep capital expenditure really low.
4. Cut operating costs with creativity and courage.
5. Spend on advertising deployment not on advertising creation.
6. Always have three cost options for every planned company purchase.
7. Pay six people the salary of eight and get them to do the job of ten.
8. Pay more for suppliers with a culture of innovation.

8

Throwing Toddlers in the Deep End

HR Lessons from Hindustan Unilever

'Take a break for a month, come back and complete the one-year management training stint. After that feel free to leave, but like a mountaineer who takes a break while climbing, quit only after you've climbed the peak.'

Our head of HR Prem Kamath's sanguine advice worked. A month after my talk with him I took back the hastily written resignation I had submitted only two months after joining HUL. I was posted in Madhya Pradesh in our foods business as a salesperson. Based in Jabalpur, I had to visit forty shops a day trying to sell Dalda and Kissan Ketchup, taking a bus to the far corners of the state, from Tikamgarh in the north to Chhindwara in the south. One evening I boarded a crowded bus from Jabalpur to Chattarpur. Two hours later the bus came to a standstill near a bridge. The curious thing about MP bridges is that they are concave and not convex: they curve in till they touch the riverbed and then rise again. This is fine eleven months of the year, but in rainy July they can flood easily.

After waiting by the bridge for three hours, I decided to retrace my steps back to Jabalpur. The next morning, I woke up to the news that a bus, not mine thankfully, had capsized on a similar concave bridge, leading to several deaths. It was the proverbial last straw. I promptly boarded a train to Mumbai and, resignation in hand, sought an appointment with Prem Kamath.

HR is HUL's secret weapon. The department has two qualities that many HR departments don't have. It has the teeth to stand up to business satraps and it has the ability to empathetically break rules the way Prem had done for me. In a chairman's speech Harish Manwani had listed six principles of the HUL way of people management – get them early, train them well, build careers, encourage diversity, reward performance and instil values. It is a pretty good way to structure this chapter.

Get Them Early = Recruit Right the First Time

Lord Cole, chairman of Unilever, visited India in 1965 and as was customary was interacting with a young manager. 'Sir, what are the criteria for appointments to the board?' the young manager asked the chairman. 'I'm glad you are thinking so far ahead,' Lord Cole replied. 'The criteria for board appointments are contribution, competence and character. The last takes precedence over the first two.'

HUL measures calibre using three criteria: judgement, drive and influence – JDI. Judgement is the ability to take the right decisions. My one-time boss Sanjay Dube is the best decision-maker I have seen. If you went to him for a decision, he would first give you an intuitive answer. He would then analyse the issue, mentally evaluate the options WAC style and give you a decision quickly. Seven out of ten times he would be right, and the three times he had got it wrong, it would be on less important issues or on issues where his intuition and logic didn't match. But seven out of ten decisions, if they are quick, is a great ratio.

Drive is the ability and desire to get things done. A lot of people work hard, but if it is not output-oriented, then it is a bias for activity and not for action. Then again there are people who are great intellectuals and spend their time fashioning a great solution, but when it is time for action they falter.

Influence is getting the world to see your point of view. One obvious technique to gain influence is through collaboration and teamwork. Playing golf with your boss is another. Or it could be analytical horsepower or lawyerly arguments, or personal charisma and charm. The point is, whatever the way, are you able to influence the decisions of others?

Drive is the most important trait in junior management,

influence in middle management and judgement at senior levels.

To evaluate calibre as measured by JDI and then character, HUL goes through a fourfold process. The CV is the best judge of drive. Looking at a candidate's academic and co-curricular achievements gives you a sense of how hard a person is willing to work towards an end. Your grades and the academic institutions you attend don't indicate your ability to judge or influence, but they certainly show drive. Similarly, a state-level cricket player or the head of a college students' association is likely to be highly driven. Sanjay Dube says, 'By and large HUL leaders are high achievers in their academic careers and the confidence that they bring because of that is reinforced by the institutional self-confidence they encounter in the company. The underlying belief is that there is nothing that cannot be done and achieved by HUL and its brands. Having seen HUL as a competitor and having seen other Unilever organizations, this is what strikes me the most about HLL leaders and its culture.'

Having shortlisted those considered highly driven candidates, HUL then conducts a group discussion. Most participants believe that they are being judged for their decibel levels or brilliant contributions. But what we are looking for is the ability to influence the group. Sure, a brilliant contribution can make a difference. But so does someone for whom the group pauses when she speaks or someone who helps another participant make a point effectively or someone who takes off and builds on the point of another participant. The level of influence a person can exert on a group discussion regardless of personality is how HUL judges influence during recruitments.

Candidates who make the cut in the group discussion are then led on to a preliminary interview with mid-level managers. The focus here is on judgement. Judgement, as we saw earlier, requires intuition and reasoning. The ability to decide sober and drunk. There are two ways to judge judgement: one is to give a problem ambiguously worded to the candidate and the other is to ask her to take you through a life decision.

I once asked a young man from IIM Calcutta to segment the market for umbrellas. 'Do you want me to segment the market or consumers, sir?' he asked. It was a brilliant example of clarifying a problem. Segmenting a market is always problematic because market segments are ultimately artificial constructs based on what manufacturers think are consumer segments.

It is wrong (though easy) to segment cars based on size since underlying drivers of size could be income, ease of driving and ease of parking. Segmenting consumers is the right way to look at it. My young friend from IIM Calcutta then went on to segment consumers for umbrellas based on their desire to use it for the sun, rain or for fashion. Depending on the weight and whether it was for dual or single usage. I was bowled over. Imagine an umbrella with two handles designed for two people!

Another simple way to judge problem-solving is by asking someone to estimate something they are likely to have no idea of. The number of unmarried people over thirty-five who wear black shoes with brown trousers, for instance. You'll get a good sense of how the candidate structures the problem. Occasionally you might get an inspired answer like Akbar got when he asked Birbal how many crows there were in Agra. '95463, sire,' was Birbal's reply. 'What if we count and there are fewer?' That only means they have gone on a holiday to a neighbouring town. 'And what if there are more?' You can guess the answer by now.

The fourth and final step in the HUL way of recruiting is an interview with a very senior manager from HUL, often a director. The purpose of this interview is to assess the candidate's character. It is hard to judge character, but a good way is to see how authentic a candidate is while responding to tough questions like 'tell us the biggest failure in your life' or 'what about yourself are you most insecure about?' Candidates who are reflective, open to sharing their vulnerabilities and honest about themselves tend to be honest in their dealings with others.

M.K. Sharma, former vice chairman of HUL and then chairman of ICICI Bank, recalls his final interview in 1974. He was asked just two questions. He had mentioned in his form that he was fluent in Sanskrit. His interviewer, Dr Ranjan Banerjee, then HR director, who also happened to be a Sanskrit scholar, recited some couplets and asked MK to translate. The next question by David Webb, then vice chairman, moved the conversation from the sublime to the profane. Had he ever watched a blue film? It was a trick question, but like the Sanskrit question one meant to test the moral compass of the candidate. I never dared ask the patrician MK what his answer had been.

Get Them Early: A Great Summer Internship Programme

Many companies treat summer training as a PR exercise, where trainees are given a good time but are not exposed to the inner workings of the company. HUL takes its summer internship programme very seriously. Perhaps it is the middle-class way of extracting the most from every employee even if they are around only for eight weeks. Each trainee is given a one-page project with a sharp problem to solve.

Solving the problem must involve meeting consumers and customers and accessing some of HUL's key business databases. Along with doing the project, trainees help their bosses with day-to-day operational work. The trainees are mainly based in Mumbai and live in a fully furnished HUL guest house and usually form lifelong bonds of friendship.

The old HUL office at Backbay Reclamation had a KGB-like feel to it, with its grey facade and socialist architecture, and the two Husain murals on the outer walls did not redeem it in any way. If it weren't for the smell of soap that pervaded the building, you could be excused for thinking that a Russian with steely grey eyes would pop out from behind the ominous closed doors and say, 'Komitet Gosudarstvennoy Bezopasnosti.' Gopal Vittal, my summer tutor, was not in the office on the first day of my internship. It was a hot summer day and after a heavy meal at the canteen I went behind the large table of the summer trainee room and plonked myself on the floor for an afternoon siesta. The unwelcoming doors ensured that we had no surprise visitors on my first official workday.

My summer project was the implementation of Project Bharat, probably the largest direct sampling programme any company in India had undertaken. The personal products division at HUL had seen rapid growth in the mid and late 1990s on the back of penetration gains of shampoo, skin creams and toothpaste in urban India. Rural penetration was however low, and the plan was to knock on village doors and sell a special Bharat pack

consisting of four personal products at a discounted price
to 16 million households. Forcing trial is a well-accepted
marketing technique to drive category adoption.

Gopal promptly dispatched me to Bihar to assess the
project pilot. Airplane travel was a rarity, and I felt like a
VIP when two HUL salespeople came to the airport to
receive me. They were a bit disappointed when the 'saheb'
from head office turned out to be a mere summer trainee.
I checked into a hotel which was akin to Hotel Decent
made famous by the Bollywood movie *Jab We Met*.

To escape the hotel restaurant, I had dinner in a
Marwari bhojanalaya that night. The bhojanalaya was
lit with paraffin lamps and a dim medieval light that
emanated from a coal fire. The food unsurprisingly was
delicious, and ever since I've sworn that when travelling
in North India the only place you will get clean food is at
a Marwari bhojanalaya near the railway station.

The next morning, I travelled with six Project Bharat
salespeople in a cramped van. Except for a few touristy
trips, this was my first experience of rural India. Our
destination was Lakshmanpur, about 10 kilometres from
the town of Aarrah, and I remember crossing the wide
and majestic Ganga. The village itself, unlike dirty Patna
and filthy Aarrah, was a hermitage from a Kalidasa play.
Coconut palms lined the road, and the mainly mud houses
were ensconced in small groves.

With some trepidation, I followed the salesperson into the first house. In sharp contrast to my own treatment of door-to-door salespeople in Mumbai, the woman was welcoming. She wanted to know what shampoo was. Would it make her hair less dry than the Lifebuoy soap she used? She spoke about how her daughter would flinch every time she ran a fine comb through her soap-washed hair. It reminded me of a scene in Satyajit Ray's *Pather Panchali*, where Sarbajaya is combing her daughter's rough hair, bemoaning the lack of oil and wondering how she would get her daughter married.

In the afternoon, after seventy door-to-door calls, we set up a television screen in the centre of the village. We were planning to show some Hindi film songs punctuated with advertisements of our products. Despite the inducement of a lucky draw, women did not want to come and watch TV in public. So we had to make do with fifty bare-torsoed children and an ancient-looking man for an audience. After the first five minutes, the shrivelled old man suddenly sprang to life and, waving his stick, roared at us to shut the TV. Shah Rukh Khan and Madhuri Dixit canoodling in *Dil to Pagal Hai* was obscene, he said. Why not show the Ramayana instead, he asked.

The heat, dust and magic of the experience, along with the seriousness accorded to my project recommendations, convinced me that HUL was indeed the place for me to work in. Twenty years later, the HUL summer training experience remains almost unaltered. In 2018 we made twenty-one offers to summer trainees to join us as full-time employees and all but two accepted.

Train Them Well: The Management Training Stint

The HUL summer internship is just a prelude to the famous management training stint. Started in 1955, the management training scheme had the express purpose of grooming future leaders to run the company. The talent was the very best in the country and, as Steve Turner, then chairman, said, they were to be 'homespun but excellently spun'.

If there is one differentiator between HUL and every other company in India, it is the totality of business exposure of the management training stint. As Sanjay Dube said, 'It's a little like compulsory military service that builds national character of discipline and integrity.' The underlying principle of the yearlong management training stint is to allow trainees to live the life of the lowest-ranking company functionary in every large department.

My own management training stint was the most formative year in my life. I spent the first sixteen weeks, punctuated with a one-month break, in central Madhya Pradesh or Mahakaushal as it is called. The sales stint was, in hindsight anyway, fun. I would get into a three-wheeler loaded with HUL's food products and visit forty shops a day with the distributor's salesperson.

In each shop we would try to get the attention of the shopkeeper and from a big register read out a list of products we wanted him to buy. If the shopkeeper demurred from buying a product, we would ask him to stock at least six units; if he asked for six units, we would convince him to take twelve. We would then clean the grimy Dalda packs in the shelf with a piece of cloth we had brought along and put up a poster of the new Rs 2 jam sachet outside the shop. The next week the poster would get torn, but no matter, we would put up another one.

Madhya Pradesh in the monsoon is beautiful. The verdant coal mines of Singrauli and the architecturally rich Bundelkhand were part of my beat. Once you got used to it there was a Zen-like peace in doing forty sales calls, a feeling of deep satisfaction at the end of a successful day and a magical journey back to the Jabalpur headquarters to look forward to.

After the sales stint I did a marketing stint on Annapoorna salt, a rural stint in Etah, which I have dwelt on, a market research stint and a factory stint. The market research stint was particularly humiliating since most people bang the door shut in your face just as you are about to introduce yourself. Having been at the receiving end, my standing instruction in my home now is to always welcome a market researcher with the bare minimum offer of water if not answers.

The stint I was most proud of was my factory stint. I wasn't an engineer and had never been to a factory except on school tours. I was sent to HUL's famous Mumbai factory, the symbol of the city's manufacturing prowess in the 1950s and 1960s. The factory had fallen on bad days recently, with the bulk of the volumes moving to more tax efficient parts of the country. The factory stint was considered a holiday stint for marketeers and my batchmate Tan and I would spend hours imitating all the wonderful characters we met on the shop floor living in a time warp. Midway through my stint, I was asked if I would help with a problem that had been perplexing the factory for the last few years, 'The Oil Loss Problem'.

During the soap-making process, some of the oil evaporates, leaks, etc., and it was permissible to lose about 0.2 per cent of oil between input and output. So for every 1000 tonnes of oil that comes into the factory, 998 tonnes has to be accounted for in soap production. Over the years the oil loss had moved from 0.2 per cent to 0.4 per cent to now 0.8 per cent. The factory manager was getting rapped hard on the knuckles by the head-office mandarins.

Like several people before me, I whipped out my

magnifying glass, so to say, and started exploring the pipes and tanks for a leak. Try as hard as I could, I just wasn't able to find any cause for the oil loss. A few days before I was to leave the factory, I got in very early in the morning and saw some tankers being weighed and leaving the factory. When I asked the shift manager what it was, he said it was distilled fatty acid (DFA), an intermediary in the oil to soap process, which was leaving for the Khamgaon factory.

An idea struck me, and I quickly looked up the volumes that were leaving the factory. For every 4000 tonnes of oil, 3000 tonnes equivalent of DFA was going to Khamgaon and only 1000 tonnes were being processed in Mumbai. Now 4000 tonnes of oil coming in will mean 8 tonnes (0.2 per cent) being lost due to normal factors. But the 3000 tonnes of DFA that was being sent to Khamgaon did not take any share in this loss.

Exactly 3000 tonnes worth was weighed and sent. In other words, the oil loss that should have been allocated to Khamgaon was all being borne by Mumbai, and Mumbai looked like it was losing 8 tonnes for the 1000 tonnes it produced. With the proportion of Khamgaon increasing over the years, the oil loss in the Mumbai factory was getting magnified. The factory manager almost kissed me when he heard that it was an accounting loss and not a real loss of oil.

There were two major lessons for me from this

experience. The first is that when numbers look outrageous, attack the numbers first before interrogating reality. The second, get to the office early. You never know what you may find.

Build Careers

From my IIMA 1999 batch there are only three people I know who are still in the company they joined from campus. Coincidentally, they all work for marquee firms famed for their HR practices: Unilever, Procter & Gamble and the Boston Consulting Group. What sets these companies apart is a structured approach to career planning and, much more importantly, a genuine commitment to building the long-term careers of its employees.

I see three principles in the HUL way of career planning: early field responsibilities; breadth in beginning, followed by depth in middle management and then breadth again at senior management; and leaders building leaders.

Start on the field

'Only factory workers and sales teams create value, rest all are overheads.' The statement, allegedly made by A.C.

Chakravarty, factory manager of the Calcutta factory, symbolizes the focus the company had on last-mile execution. No leaders progressed without going through the leadership crucibles of factories and sales stints. Sanjay Dube says this did two things. It built rapport between front-line teams and top leaders, which was critical for building strategies that weren't written in ivory towers and it raised the profile of these functions within the organization, which is critical for motivation and morale in these lonely, repetitive assignments.

As a consequence, the first job in HUL is almost always a field leadership job: as an area sales manager, a factory finance manager, a factory engineer or a branch HR manager. My first job after management training was as an ASM for soaps and detergents in Madhya Pradesh. I had a team of twenty direct subordinates and several hundred distributors and distributor salespeople who saw me, a gawky twenty-four-year-old, as head of the family. **The rules of leadership are the same everywhere. Initial scepticism turns to adoration if and only if the officer can do his core job better than his men and women.** In this case it was sales.

Selling more in a shop than the sales executive was good, but it was expected. In MP there was an unwritten rule that when the ASM visited an outlet, the shopkeeper did not say no to an order. Chandan, the biggest trader in

Jabalpur, reminded me when I was trying to sell something to him, *'ASM saab se mujhe dhandhe ki baat karne ki himmat nahin hai'* (I don't want to speak business with ASM saab).

To win the respect of my people, I had to do something more. In those days, Nirma had made a deep foray into the soaps category, stealing a lot of market share. MP was one of the key markets for Nirma. HUL's counter was Breeze soap, but try as we did Breeze never crossed 10 per cent of Nirma. Unlike HUL, which believed in distributing in every small shop, Nirma sold to 250 wholesalers, from whom the other shopkeepers bought.

I invited 250 wholesalers from across MP, along with their wives, to a five-star hotel in Khajuraho. Most had never stayed in a five-star hotel, or taken a non-religious holiday. One of them told me that he had seen a bathtub only in Lux films and found it much better for amorous pursuits than the bed in his room.

In the evening after some variety entertainment I opened an auction for Breeze. I had negotiated a low price for Breeze that day with the brand manager. Wholesalers sat at round tables district-wise. The auction began and in every round the wholesaler raised his stakes in terms of cartons of Breeze he would buy. The district winner was given a prize and made to compete in a zonal table. The three zonal winners came on stage and competed in an all-MP round. The only rule was that the wholesaler would have to lift the cartons he had committed to regardless of whether or not he won the auction. The presence of their wives, spirits and a city feeling ensured that we sold in one night what we would normally sell in ten months. The back of Nirma in MP was broken. Of course, despite these initial successes, as I have mentioned earlier in the chapter on sales management, it didn't build Breeze in MP, but it did make me a hero to my men.

Another HUL alumnus who has become CEO, Anand Kripalu, of United Spirits and Diageo in India, recalls the tremendous impact his sales stint had on him. Posted first in Tamil Nadu and then UP, he had to take a train on Sunday nights to a market and work the week with his front-line salesperson in the deep hinterland. Six days in a row – first sales call to last sales call. The empathy and insight that this foundational experience gave him were key to him as he rose in his career first as CEO for Cadbury India and now at Diageo.

Harish Manwani says the HUL sales system has such a competitive advantage because we have traditionally placed our brightest people in sales. No matter which IIT or IIM you came from, your first job was always on the field. It gave you a real grounding but at the same time ensured a leading-edge sales system. Harish recalls his batchmate Mickey Pant who had joined from one of the IITs straight into sales. They had a meeting to decide where to build a sales depot for a state. Mickey cut a large map of the state, stuck it on a cardboard sheet and placed small stones on the board in proportion to where the sales in the state were coming from. He then took a pivot and said wherever on the map the pivot balanced the board was where a depot should be built. Harish remembers it as an example of a brilliant mind working on the most common of problems.

The right breadth and depth

After a field stint, managers usually move to a head-office stint. Between these two stints lasting about six years, the company usually makes up its mind on the potential of the employee, and unknown to the manager serious career planning begins. As already mentioned, the stated principle is breadth early, depth in middle management and breadth again in senior management.

Let me take the example of Nitin Paranjpe, currently COO of Unilever and one of HUL's most successful products. After a spell as an ASM in UP, Nitin was made brand manager of the Vim scouring powder. During his long and successful stint, he was identified as a high-potential talent. He was sent back as the branch manager for the South branch, where he handled a major retailer strike in Kerala. He was then made a member of

Project Millennium, a high-profile project to reimagine HUL for the twenty-first century. From here he moved for a short London assignment as executive assistant to the Unilever chairman and then came back to head the homecare (detergents and dish-wash) business in India for several years. He then got promoted to Home and Personal Care director before being promoted to CEO HUL. This is a classic case of adding portfolio to high performing managers, ensuring at the same time continuity, fresh challenges and career progression. After an extremely impactful tenure as CEO, Nitin was promoted to the Unilever Executive as president for Home Care globally, followed by a short stint as president Foods and Refreshments and now COO. All of HUL's career planning principles are at work here – early field stint, high potential identification at an early but not infant stage of one's career, depth in a business (homecare) with periodic additional responsibilities, followed by senior management breadth.

Leaders build leaders

The third and most important principle in career building is that leaders build leaders, with generations of leaders committed to nurturing the next round of leaders. By the time a manager has spent seven to ten years in HUL, there is broad consensus on whether he has top potential, and one or two leaders invest serious time and effort on the employee.

Nitin Paranjpe remembers how Keki Dadiseth, then director for detergents, would invite him, a junior brand manager, to be a fly on the wall in meetings with corporate heavyweights. Sanjay Dube, a mid-career recruit, remembers how Shunu Sen, head of marketing, would meet him every two weeks for a mentorship contact.

Anuradha Razdan, HR director, says that the abiding principle in leadership development is 70:20:10 – 70 per cent of development is by a leader building a leader on the job, 20 per cent formal coaching interventions by the boss and 10 per cent in the classrooms by external faculty.

R. Gopalakrishnan remembers his favourite leadership lesson. As a young manager in 1969, Gopalakrishnan attended the farewell of then chairman P.L. Tandon. After the party, P.L. Tandon was being ushered to his chauffeur-driven Dodge car. He politely declined to get in and said that now that he had retired he would prefer to drive his own Fiat back home. The incident made a deep impact on the young manager. Several years later, when Gopalakrishnan was retiring, P.L. Tandon asked him if he could give some unsolicited advice. 'Working life is like a play,' he said. 'When the curtains are drawn, never come back to the stage unless you are specifically invited.' A great example of learning by seeing and a formal coaching intervention decades apart.

Encourage Diversity

When I was in college, I read an article in the *Economic Times* on the characteristics of an HUL manager: aggressive, analytical and action-oriented. When asked whether HUL was producing clones, a senior manager said, 'Yes, but very good ones at that.' R. Gopalakrishnan says that HUL's leadership planning has an excellent filtering process, but it turns out particles of roughly the same size. These do very well under stable conditions, but in periods of extreme volatility HUL tends to get on the back foot for some time.

Let us be frank. Diversity is not perceived as one of HUL's strengths. Several (though it is now changing) of its directors are typically management trainees who have spent over twenty years or more in the company. Most HUL lifers tend to have the qualities mentioned in the *Economic Times* and come from similar educational and social backgrounds. When I went to the UK for a three-year stint, I was surprised to find that unlike in HUL, where every social interaction continues to be a business discussion, lunches in our London canteen were conspicuously non-work-centred.

The company has taken a much more conscious call over gender diversity. The business case for having many more women managers in a business where most consumers are women is strong. HUL saw that while at intake the gender balance was 50:50, by the time it came to middle management the ratio became highly tilted in favour of men. A study identified that post-delivery many women find it hard to come back to work. Three big interventions that HUL made were a liberal maternity policy, with six months' fully paid leave, a 5000 square foot day-care centre on campus and a career by choice programme, where mid-career women are encouraged to come back and work with flexi timings. This has resulted in the proportion of women in the workforce going up from 11 per cent a decade ago to 40 per cent in 2018.

There is however an area of diversity where HUL has been world class for a long time: the tolerance and even encouragement of mavericks. In most companies there is a trinity of professionals: Mavericks, Company Men and Rogues. Mavericks are the creators. They tend to be weak team players, rebellious but also genuine value creators and people with very high integrity. Company Men are rigorous, loyal, process-driven team players, who also exhibit high integrity. Rogues are high energy, creative and achievement-oriented but put short-term self-interest ahead of long-term company goals. They are the destroyers of companies.

The CEO Factory

In many big organizations Mavericks are sidelined early and the battle to climb the corporate ladder is between the Company Men and the Rogues. Alok Kshirsagar, a senior partner with a top consulting firm, says that this sidelining of Mavericks happens because many big companies overemphasize collaboration at the expense of great outcomes. Collaboration is not the strong suit of Mavericks.

HUL is slightly different. Its performance orientation along with deep-seated values of integrity and an esprit de corps formed in tough early stints means two things. Company Men always beat the Rogues to the top. The few Rogues that get past the crack usually get caught out at middle management. Mavericks rarely make it to the very top, but you will find them at every level including just below the top. Their reward for creating discontinuous value is that they are remembered for decades in the oral folklore of the company.

Reward Performance

Performance management forms the backbone of any professional company. A weak performance culture is a long-term recipe for disaster, but an ultra-strong performance culture makes heroes and villains too quickly, encourages short-termism and discourages collaboration.

200

As mentioned in chapter one, HUL has a 'supportive meritocracy' where HUL picks, identifies and builds a leadership pipeline based on performance and nurtures these leaders when they face difficult circumstances. HUL's performance management system has three pillars.

An objective goal for performance

HUL is relatively lucky in that at senior levels its managers can easily be judged by the sales revenue and profit they bring in along with a few measures on capability development and social impact. Many but not all organizations have this. For instance, an uncle of mine who became cabinet secretary half-jokingly said that he had an edge since his ranking in the UPSC examination thirty years ago was higher than that of the other candidates! Where HUL is unique is in its ability to design simple input metrics that can judge the quality of results of its middle and junior management staff. If overall growth is good, it could be due to markets growing faster and so market share is an important metric. Market share could be due to a great product a predecessor could have launched and so the quality of advertising done in the current year (as measured in a market research test) is the better metric for the current year. You can grow and win market share and yet be rated poorly in a year if the quality of advertising you personally were responsible for is poor.

Hemant Bakshi has written about the time he, as a brand manager, was in the middle of a big competitive battle with a rival much bigger in the category he was working on. He asked his boss what goals of performance he should set for himself. His boss gave him three goals: the CEO of the competitor should be fired; they should sell their head office; their factories should become so empty that HUL products should be made in them. Hemant tells me his boss was only half-joking.

A system that measures and rates

At Unilever everyone has a 3 + 1 goal set at the beginning of the year. Three business goals and one personal development goal. At the end of the year the manager is rated not by his boss alone but by a functional resource committee (FRC) on these goals. The FRC consists of his boss, his boss's peers and his boss's boss. All in all, about eight people judging a group of thirty to forty managers. Each case is discussed for a good twenty to thirty minutes. Were the goals appropriately challenging, was there a context to the achievement or lack of it and how does the performance compare with that of others in the peer set? Each manager is rated on a scale of 1 to 5 for the current year's performance such that the average rating of all the candidates in the pool is approximately 3. A few years ago, it was exactly 3, but to end silly discussions going on into the wee hours of the night, it was changed to approximately 3!

Hemant Bakshi was a master at running fair FRCs. He was usually quite jovial and casual, but on the FRC meeting morning he would be cool and distant. He would have consolidated an Excel sheet with all the objectives, colour coded achievements and proposed ratings. He would start off with candidates he felt were proposed at a higher rating than they deserved. He would give his views, the candidate's manager would passionately defend her employee and the other managers sitting there would generally subtly concur with Hemant's view, since a lower rating for one candidate in the pool would mean a potentially higher rating for someone in their team (remember ratings were normalized to 3).

If occasionally Hemant couldn't decide, he would come back to the candidate at the end of the FRC meeting and look at the spread of the ratings. He believed that while it was comfortable for us to rate the whole pool around 3 with very little deviation, we had to give a clear signal to top performers and weak performers. There would be acrimonious debates on the three managers who should get a 5 rating, knowing fully well that for every 5 rating there would be a corresponding 1 rating. We would then come back to the one we couldn't decide on, and Hemant would now be the decision-maker. It was tense, since careers were made on this decision. I once chased Hemant into the men's loo along with a few colleagues to force him to reverse a rating decision. It was a wise move since after a long day the urgency of the call of nature usually wins over the propriety of the calls of duty.

Promotions based on ratings and not biases

While current-year bonuses are entirely based on ratings, promotions are based primarily on potential. It is all very well to have a great process to evaluate talent, but if at the time of promotions, you promote your drinking buddy on the grounds of potential that is the end of meritocracy. In all honesty, HUL can do better here, though on balance the best do tend to rise to the top.

An assessment of potential in deciding promotions is subjective and while the HR department does a formal assessment of potential, the final say in a candidate's selection rests with the line manager and at most with the line manager's manager. That is why HUL periodically gets it wrong on promotions. But, as mentioned in chapter one, HUL gets it right more often than not because its HR department with its functional reporting is a powerful entity that can independently convene interviews to review a candidate's poor performance record. Also, HUL's batch system for promotions, though it has its critics, broadly works.

Just like promotions, decisions to ask a candidate to leave the organization are also taken objectively.

Asha Gopalakrishnan, vice president finance, gives a great example. 'We were in an FRC looking to disengage a manager for poor performance. We were struggling to come to a decision because while we were clear that the performance was sub-par, he was not only a very likeable person, but also had a few personal issues, which losing a job would exacerbate. Balaji [the CFO] helped us get clarity by asking us to "take the decision to separate someone with absolute ruthlessness, with only the interest of the company. But execute the action with full empathy and compassion – if this means giving a long notice, outplacement support, etc., do it and land it in a way that does not impact his self-esteem." It helped us separate the decision and the emotion, and take the right decision and execute it in a humane way.'

Instil values

The final principle of the HUL HR system is to instil values. Values are so key to HUL's success that it deserves a chapter by itself. The final and most important chapter of this short book. As a sample of what you will see more of in the next chapter, here's a great anecdote.

Anandi Shankar, currently general manager HR for GSK's proposed merger with HUL, was till recently heading sales HR. In 2018 a company sales officer was found guilty of financial embezzlement on a Friday and asked to leave that very day. He requested for permission to continue for one more day so that he could come in and hand over his belongings and make a full and final settlement with the company. Unfortunately, on the weekend, he met with a serious accident and was hospitalized. Unsure what to do, Anandi called her boss, the HR director Dinesh Biddappa, who said that an 'employee is *our* employee till he is our employee'. HUL moved him to a better hospital, flew down his family and stationed someone in the hospital throughout the period. Sadly, he didn't make it and HUL managed his funeral expenses and expedited the entire benefits he would have been entitled to.

The HR systems at HUL have contributed more than anything else into making callow, young trainees into future

CEOs. Let us quickly summarize the main learnings from this chapter before moving to the last chapter.

Summary

1. Good recruitment of candidates is more than half the job done. Character and calibre are key.
2. Judge calibre by underlying competencies of judgement, drive and influence, and character through a very senior manager interview.
3. The underlying principle of management training is to allow trainees to live the life of the lowest-ranking company functionary in every department.
4. Early field responsibilities in either factories or sales are a must.
5. Breadth in early stages, depth in middle levels and breadth again at senior levels is an HUL principle of career development.
6. Only leaders can build other leaders. Work with people who are committed to your development however harsh they may seem.
7. Encourage diversity both in form (gender, nationality, etc.) and in terms of thought. HUL's encouragement of mavericks has been a key factor in its success.
8. Always have simple, measurable, actionable goals for performance.

9. Objectively judge candidates on performance. Reward current-year for performance, but make sure potential enters the conversation when planning promotions.
10. Take people decisions in the interest of the company, but execute them with full empathy and compassion.

9

From Great to Good

Values at Hindustan Unilever

A Business Governed by Conscience

Anand Kripalu feels that the difference between a company and an institution is that the latter is defined by a purpose much larger than profit. An institution is built brick by brick, with 'values' being the cement that binds it together. HUL, Kripalu says, is an institution in the true sense.

Creating brands, businesses and people with purpose remains at the very heart of Unilever and, as a consequence, of HUL. Our big brands Dove, Lifebuoy, Surf Excel and Brooke Bond Red Label all have recognizable powerful purposes at their heart, be it improving self-esteem of women or encouraging kids to have a freer childhood or making India more inclusive or reducing diarrhoea-related deaths. These brands are among our most successful and there is plenty of long- and short-term data to suggest that purpose has driven these brands.

Most simply, brands that are authentically purposeful

get remembered more, as we have seen in the marketing chapter. The path to purposeful brands is difficult and full of thorns. Difficult because the purpose of the brand has to be deeply rooted in the genetic history of the brand and linked to the category. Consumers smell bullshit from a distance.

Full of thorns because periodically purposeful brands are subject to greater scrutiny and attack from sections of society. In the past year I myself have seen two massive negative Twitter reactions to Brooke Bond Red Label films. Our principle is simple. If we have knowingly or unknowingly hurt sentiments, we apologize, but if we believe we are in the right, we will persist.

Purpose is not just a slogan at Unilever or something that only the corporate social responsibility department must deal with. All managers above a certain seniority have sustainability-linked targets as part of their annual performance indicators. I, for instance, have a metric called 'percent tea sourced sustainably' as a metric that drives my bonus payout.

HUL, along with its main competitor Tata Tea, helped set up a body called Trustea that certifies plantations on whether they employ sustainable agricultural practices, pay fair wages and ensure good living conditions of its labour. From zero per cent a few years ago, this number has risen to 65 per cent in 2018. The target for 2019 is to make it 75 per cent. There are several other hard sustainability targets that senior managers in HUL carry – percentage of food that is compliant with the highest nutritional standards, percentage of plastic that HUL uses which is recyclable, water and carbon emissions from a factory, etc. In true HUL style, these targets have to be measured, tracked and rewarded.

Brands and businesses will only be purpose-driven if the values of the people driving them are purpose-driven. Let us look at the values that most HUL managers seem to share.

Is Values Just Management Speak?

Every business, small or big, has value statements. Enron, for example, had the photographs depicting their values of respect, integrity, communication and excellence framed all over their offices. Even if not in flagrant violation of the law like Enron, very few companies live up to their values under pressure, and certainly not for a very long period.

Around two decades ago, HUL was going through a very tough phase of business. During an annual chairman's review, Vindi Banga identified one of the causes of our poor performance as a deviation from the four values that had built HUL – action, courage, caring and truth (ACCT). We youngsters in the last row rolled up our eyes and sniggered.

Typical senior management escapism. The business is burning and here we are exchanging mealy-mouthed platitudes. We had great fun at the expense of ACCT. If someone left the lunch table before others finished, we would say no caring. If someone was staring blankly at the computer screen, we'd say where is the action. And the value of truth was often facetiously changed into beauty, peace and other words associated with the Buddha.

Values in the context of a business have no meaning unless they have a clear impact on business outcomes over a long period of time and unless they are lived by most employees. It is not important whether employees remember verbatim the company's official values. Much more important is that when asked to articulate them, most employees say roughly the same thing.

While researching this book, I asked several alumni and current managers for memorable HUL stories. I was hoping for stories from the trenches, of battles won and businesses conquered. Instead what I got was a series of stories on values. Even when I pushed my respondents to focus on business successes, there was always a 'values' moral at the end of the story. Two things surprised me about the stories. The best stories were repeated by different generations of Leverites and, as I clustered these stories, I realized they fell neatly into four buckets – action, courage, caring and truth.

I was perplexed. Values are easy to frame but extremely difficult to implement across the length and breadth of the company. How did a company as large and as old as HUL manage to have such uniformity in value systems across the company? Why were the stories on values repeating themselves?

My grandfather had published a book called the *Children's Ramayana*, which he read to his grandchildren every night. He would not read it chronologically but repeat his favourite few stories every few nights – Rama fulfilling his father's vow, Bharata placing Rama's shoes on the throne and the complex morality of the killing of Vali.

Perhaps that was the answer to HUL's unique value system. Stories that become folklore of people, especially senior leadership, who have lived the values through generations. The stories self-reinforcing themselves with every generation may well be the answer to HUL's famed value system.

Action

At the same chairman's review, Vindi said something that has remained with me. 'The only thing that matters,' he said in his gravelly voice, 'is not what we think or say but how we act.' A bias for action at a collective level is one of the great traits of HUL. Gopal Vittal calls it a rare quality of 'entrepreneurial professionalism', where ownership of the company is so high among employees that they act even without required permissions.

On the face of it, however, action orientation is far from a strength at HUL. Younger managers will gripe about how slow we are and a score called 'bias for action' usually scores very poorly in company surveys. Day-to-day activities can get caught in a maze of processes. God help you if you want to change your laptop or register a new vendor in the system. But when there is a crisis the bias for action has to be seen to be believed.

Arun Adhikari recalls an instance of how HUL in times of emergency gears into high speed action. The bits of wool that stick out of sweaters is called bobbling and it is common in many fabrics but especially woollens. In the winter of 1998, P&G was about to launch Ariel with anti-bobbling properties.

Arun and his marketing manager laundry, Rohit Jawa, got to know of this launch on 23 December. Surf Excel had just won a bruising leadership battle against Ariel, and Arun was paranoid this would turn the clock back. Arun called Unilever R&D in the UK, where everyone was just about to go on Christmas leave. Did they have anything in the arsenal for bobbling?

The folks in the UK replied that there was an enzyme called clazinaze which helped in reducing bobbling, and

Unilever in Brazil had just used it in their detergent. 'Goodbye, good luck and see you in the New Year,' they said, hanging up. Arun immediately called Brazil and heard they had some extra clazinaze in stock. It was instantly airfreighted to India, but there were two problems. One, a new ingredient in a detergent needs to go through a storage test of twelve weeks; and second, the factory in Chhindwara had a dosing facility for only two enzymes, both of which were already being used. Manual dosing of enzymes was out of the question since it was a safety hazard. There were some rules that could not be broken.

The R&D team under Dr Dhanuka simulated conditions to give a storage test in four weeks and they came up with the idea of creating an enzyme cocktail at the supplier's end so that only two dosing stations would be required. The product was in the market by the end of January: only four weeks after P&G had launched theirs. They may have even cracked the deadline had it not been for the ad – it was washing and drying the sweater used in the advertisement fifty times for it to bobble that caused the delay.

Shiva Krishnamurthy, vice president foods, says HUL's all-pervasive 'can-do' spirit is a fuel for its execution machinery. He recalls an incident that happened recently, where an impossible business task had been set and all eyes were on the supply chain planner, Rakesh Jha. With an air of inevitability, Rakesh gallantly said, '*Shaadi ka card chhap chuka hai . . . ab toh karna hi padega.*' (The wedding card has already been printed, we have to go through with the wedding.)

It will strike a chord with many of us that senior management often asks for ideas from junior management to appear democratic but rarely acts on those ideas. In 2001 Anuradha Razdan was HR manager in the West branch when the Gujarat earthquake struck. The company was seriously engaged in supporting those impacted. Anu recalls how during a young managers' interaction with Vindi Banga she made a suggestion on how the company could take a slightly different approach. She left thinking she wouldn't hear about that again, but a few weeks later at the annual chairman's review she heard a voice behind her: 'Anuradha.' It was Vindi himself and he came up to her and said, 'We heard you last week and this is what we are going to do about it.' Anu says an enduring lesson has been that if one feels strongly about something and doesn't hesitate to speak up, at HUL things will get done. Vindi himself recollects the same incident, saying that instead of contributing to the Prime Minister's Relief Fund, HUL went on to take direct responsibility for rebuilding two villages.

Surprisingly, HUL's bias for action goes hand in hand with extremely high process orientation and rigour. Anand

Kripalu remembers how his then boss, V. Kasturirangan, made him write a promotion proposal for soap to be given free with toothpaste six times before he approved it. Every single activity in HUL has set guidelines and processes that have been finessed over the years. Often it can be quite painful. But in times of crisis it is the liberating rigour that brings clarity. Often the devil is in the detail. And it helps an organization to move fast without tripping.

Courage

Courage is the ability to take the right decisions even in the face of high risk. Risks can be to one's personal career or to the business. It means speaking truth to power.

Keki Dadiseth says that in the early 1980s, as financial controller, he opposed a consignment of exports of 20,000 tonnes (massive) of detergent to Russia, since he felt that there was no market for this product and that it constituted a financial risk. The vice chairman of the company, Gerry Alcock, who was keen to hit his year-end targets, asked Keki to withdraw his objections. Keki refused, saying that Alcock had no business putting pressure on the financial controller.

Alcock dragged him to the chairman, who asked Keki to apologize for his intemperate language. Keki refused and stormed out for a midday drink to the

Bombay Gymkhana, where he got a call to go back to the chairman's room. Expecting a serious reprimand, Keki went back, only to find himself getting praised by the chairman for doing the right thing and sticking by it.

If Keki's example is one of personal courage, here's one on corporate courage that several people who spoke to me brought up. HUL was severely tested when the managers of its Doom Dooma factory in Assam were threatened by a militant organization in 1991. HUL decided not to bow down to the irrational demands of the militant group and airlifted all its managers and their families from the area. The factory was shut down at a significant cost to the company. HUL restarted operations only after law and order had been restored, and, importantly, the right to manage its operations was re-established. A decade later when there was another threat by ULFA militants, then chairman, Vindi Banga, organized army protection and suggested that the families of employees leave the factory. He recalls how all family members refused the offer saying if it was safe for their husbands, it was safe for them.

The relaunch of Lifebuoy in 2002 was one of the bravest decisions the company ever took. Lifebuoy accounted for 15 per cent of the company's turnover and was in serious decline. Led by Sanjay Dube and Gopal Vittal in a Narasimha Rao–Manmohan Singh–type team, the relaunch overturned all that Lifebuoy had stood for, for over a hundred years. In a presentation titled the 'Red Whore', Gopal and team argued that all that was good in Lifebuoy had been stripped in the quest for profits and all that remained was out of date with the consumer: the fragrance, the carbolic formulation, the pack size and the communication.

Gopal recalls how, despite all the consumer testing, the sword of 'New Coke' (where Coke famously changed its recipe based on consumer testing and had to face a major consumer backlash as a consequence) was hanging over the team. Vindi Banga, then chairman, looked Gopal squarely in the eye and asked him, 'Are you sure this will work?' 'I am absolutely, passionately convinced it will work,' replied Gopal. The project got a go-ahead and a brand that would have been consigned to the dustbin of history had a rebirth, eventually becoming one of Unilever's most important brands.

Caring

Caring was the area on which I got the most stories while researching this book. The most touching was the one Mrs Neelam Narayan related to me.

April 26, 1993 was a day when my life changed completely. I had been waiting for my husband, Prem, who had gone to Aurangabad for a conference, to return home. Around 1 o'clock I was wondering if the children and I should have lunch. So I called up Indian Airlines to find out if the flight had landed. And I was told, '*Uska toh crash ho gaya,* madam.' You know, I found it difficult to believe, so I thought that it might have been a forced landing, or it didn't take off.

So I called up Mira Singh, Gurdeep Singh's [Gurdeep was a former director at HUL] wife. Because I knew Gurdeep was on the flight. And she came to the phone, and I could tell that she must have been crying. But she had spoken to Gurdeep, and he sounded like he was all right. But he had also told her that there was a lot of smoke, and they were still looking for one another, but for me it was very reassuring that if Gurdeep was OK then everyone should be fine.

Then I called up the office. I spoke to Narendra Nanda and John Pinto. And I thought I was the person telling them about the accident, but they were already aware, and they said that they were with Mr Dutta [then chairman] and somebody will come to you just now. Very soon after that, people started coming to our home, Aloo Dadiseth, Bala Sharma, a lot of our friends, ladies, managers from the office. And for a while I was wondering what the fuss was, because I was still so sure that they would be able to find Prem.

That night I remember we had everyone sitting there. I remember Keki [Dadiseth] holding my hand and reassuring me. I think everyone knew that he had not survived, but nobody was able to tell me.

I continued to stay in Bombay with the children, although I had absolutely no family here. Mainly because of the company and the huge support that I had. In the beginning there had been a lot of hand-holding, they took care as things fell into place and I was able to grasp a little more about finance, and managing things on my own, and managing a career as well.

With their help we planned and thought out the future. And were able to start moving forward and letting go of the umbilical cord. A lot of our friends have moved away, but the support that I was given, and the confidence building in myself that happened because of all the help has made me much more independent. We decided to stay in Bombay because I could still get support from the company. And in moments like these, besides the efficiency and necessities, we talk about the HUL family. And that's been the experience. We are part of the HUL family. And family is all about care, and dignity and love and compassion and having time for each other, and that's how it has been.

There are some individual instances that I will talk about that really stood out and have helped us move forward.

So in this time of utter anguish and despair and sadness, when we could have plunged into a feeling of complete hopelessness or helplessness, I have received a lot of care from HUL. Again, as I said, I think they pre-empted what my requirements would be and with a lot of empathy and compassion again took care of many things. I guess in such cases financial help is what is a big necessity, and they started me on a pension including the medical facilities as we had earlier. I continued to use our residence, they set up a trust with the insurance money, with the trustee from HUL and myself. This was for the education of our children, so that we could invest the amount to take care of their future.

The involvement of HUL, HLL at that time, was immediate and complete. My children were very young at that time, my older son Rohan was twelve, and Varun was just six, and because they took care of everything I could be with the children. When there is loss of life there is so much that needs to be done. They managed all the rituals, the formalities, the ceremonies, legal issues, bringing Prem back from Aurangabad. And someone was at our place all the time, food was sent for I think almost two weeks, a roster had been set up, a lot of our friends were completely involved, and Dr Parekh used to be around with his care and his humour. There was a lot of warmth, and empathy, and nurturing, not just efficiency.

Mr T. Thomas had noticed how distraught Rohan was on the day of the cremation. And that very evening Mr Thomas wrote a letter to Rohan which was a turning point for him. This gave a lot of hope to Rohan and I think just realizing that this experience is not just of our own, and many others have gone through it. Another person who helped us a lot was M.K. Sharma. He has always been accessible, his advice, his legal counselling, is available at any time for any help that I wanted. He was also one of our trustees. I really am so grateful to him for that, because when one is alone and doesn't have access one can feel quite lost and vulnerable. Another personal friend of ours, John Pinto – he was a finance person – he gave a lot of advice on investments, and insisted that we bought certain shares and today they have stood me in good stead. Naren Nanda, Gurdeep – Gurdeep has always been there, he was Prem's boss at that time, and in fact was sitting next to him on the plane. And over these twenty-six years Gurdeep and the family, Meera, have always included us. I have felt like family, they are always interested in knowing how the children are doing and how I am doing.

I think everybody has been so helpful and given us so

much strength and the house was always a cheerful place even though we had lost Prem it was an irreplaceable loss but there was hope and I am very grateful to the company for that.

Letter of T. Thomas to Rohan Narayan
on 28 April 1993

My Dear Rohan,

You don't know me at all. Therefore, it is with some hesitation that I decided to write this letter, especially since you and your family are under great stress at this time. On the other hand when I saw you this morning at the crematorium asking questions of your mother while grieving for your dear father, I wanted to come and put my arms around you and comfort you by telling you how much it reminded me of something similar that I had to face at about your age – when everything seemed to have been lost and no one and nothing could console me. But I checked myself because I would probably have broken down myself along with you. So intense was what I felt for you and your brother and your mother, especially for you. You are old enough to realise the immensity of your loss; yet your span of experience is too short to

---

have prepared you for anything of this magnitude. So I thought I would write and share with you my experience in a somewhat similar situation, if only to assure you that however dark things may appear now, there is a life beyond all this tragedy both for you and for you dear ones including your father. If he could see you today that is probably what he would tell you.

You father was not only an intelligent and diligent manager, but also a very good man. Because of his goodness you as a family are blessed and you will overcome the grief and do what he would have wanted and hoped for you. I am saying this on the basis of my experience.

When I was 14, just older than what you are now, my father passed away after a stroke. It all happened in 2 or 3 days and quite unexpectedly. We had nothing in the world except some debts and my mother has 6 of us. Most people gave up hope about us. But it was my father's goodness combined with my mother's devotion and determination that gave us the courage and ability to overcome our loss and do even better than what he would have hoped for. God really blessed us because of his goodness. And so will he bless you and your family. Believe this and go forward; be a comfort to your mother who will miss your father more than anyone else. With you and your brother, she will do all that Premnarayan had dreamed for you. God will give her the strength.

If anytime you feel like talking to someone who is more like a grandfather to you, give me a call.

With my warmest regards,

Affectionately,

T. Thomas

* TT had retired as chairman, HUL, in 1980.

Stories like Mrs Narayan's abound in the company. Sudhanshu Vats recalls how when one of his salespeople in Calcutta had a heart attack, the company broke all policies to ensure he was treated in the best hospital in the city. Unfortunately, he passed away. The head of sales, Raju Aneja, came down from Mumbai and visited the bereaved family. On noticing that the family was not fully settled, he requested Sudhanshu to interview the man's son for a job but said to take him only if he is '90 per cent as good as someone you will normally take'.

M.K. Sharma talked about the case of Damodar Rathi, who drowned while at a beach in Mumbai. When he went to the house of the bereaved, he perceived a risk in terms of financial security and children's education if they were obliged to move back to their native village in remote Rajasthan. When he reported this to then chairman Ashok Ganguly, Dr Ganguly immediately said that the company must provide a flat to Mrs Rathi, alongside ring-fencing her children's education. There were reservations in the board, who protested that this would set a bad precedent, but Dr Ganguly overrode those objections and ensured that the family got a flat.

Care in HUL manifests itself best in times of personal crisis, but it also manifests in a style of leadership called 'tough love'. Anand Kripalu recalls how his boss V. Kasturirangan would be brutal through the year to his employees, but at the end of the year Anand knew he would be fairly appraised and if something went wrong professionally Kas would have his back.

I think if care is best manifested in how we treat our employees in times of crisis, an area of care we have been remiss in has been in the treatment of our distributors in some phases of our history. I remember one such phase, where we were putting a lot of pressure on our distributors to sell salt. I went to a distributor's house in Vijayawada and was embarrassed to find that he had removed a lot of the furniture in his hall to make space for the excess salt bags we had sent him. We were sitting on heaps of salt bags, the tea and biscuits were laid out on bags designed as a table and the TV was placed on a heap of salt bags. But he was too dignified and old a distributor to complain.

Truth

Generic as they sound, the bias for action, the loyalty that caring engenders and courageous decisions have all helped HUL remain successful for decades. But I think the one defining value that has determined HUL's success has been truth and its Siamese twin, integrity.

Let's start with business integrity. India is a tough environment to operate in with external business integrity. Many companies justify graft outside the company but not inside. But integrity is a slippery slope and once you're on the wrong side of it external demands are endless. Once you give in externally, standards of integrity slip inside. M.K. Sharma gave me an example of a demand that despite not being graft HUL stood up to. During the Emergency a prominent Delhi politician demanded that companies give a 5 per cent discount to consumers based in the capital city. He justified it saying that the cost of living in Delhi was high. This was not strictly graft; it was not unknown for products to have different prices in different parts of the country and many multinationals acquiesced. HUL flatly refused, since it followed a policy of uniform all-India pricing of its products, and was darkly told that it would have to bear the consequences. The next week HUL's Delhi branch was raided by the tax authorities for seven full days. On the seventh day a minor discrepancy to the tune of Rs 70 of excess recovery of sales tax (which too had been paid to the government) was found in the books of accounts. The branch manager and the finance manager were arrested.

HUL's lawyers told the police that this was an offence for which the punishment was a fine and police would have to bear the consequences of a wrongful arrest. The police asked for a bail amount of Rs 75,000, a large amount in 1975, and an impossible amount to get in the middle of the night. The distributor network was mobilized and HUL stockists arrived cash in hand to help release the two brave managers. Action, courage, caring and above all truth in one story.

But truth goes well beyond business integrity. It also means accepting wrongdoing and facing the consequences chin up. In 1999, with the acquisition of Ponds India, HUL acquired a thermometer plant in Kodaikanal. Now thermometers are not part of HUL's core business and plans were afoot to divest the plant, when news was received that in breach of company regulations glass scrap with residual mercury had been sold to a scrap dealer a few kilometres away. HUL immediately closed the factory, got the scrap back to its land and launched an investigation.

The total glass scrap was 5.4 tonnes and it contained only 7.5 kilos of mercury residue.

Several independent studies confirmed that there had been no adverse impact on the health of the employees or the environment though there had been some soil contamination within HUL's premises where the mercury had been kept. Despite having an extremely credible case of workers' health not being impacted at all, HUL made ex gratia payments to workers while at the same time not succumbing to unreasonable demands of worker associations.

Similarly, HUL has committed to clean up the site at a huge cost, which many companies would shy away from incurring, given that the factory has been shut for two decades and repeated studies have shown that the mercury content is so low that even if the soil were not remediated it would lead to neither any ecological disaster nor damage to life. Dev Bajpai, executive director legal, says that HUL could have sidestepped the issue, de-prioritized it or cut corners; instead, as usual, they chose the harder right than the easier wrong.

Dev remembers another instance he is proud of. In 2012 Unilever decided to make an open offer to acquire HUL shares from the public to increase its shareholding from 52 per cent to 75 per cent. Harish Manwani, then COO of Unilever, should have been party to this decision, but since he was also chairman of HUL, in keeping with propriety, he was kept completely in the dark.

How HUL Works

I want to conclude this book with a Zen-like story that M.K. Sharma told me. It captures the essence of HUL in many ways.

In 1975 soaps and vanaspati were under price control, making HUL a loss-making company. HUL launched a new brand of premium soap, Supreme, which didn't come under the ambit of price control. Rustomjee, an elderly sales manager handling MP East, had sent his distributors a note asking them to hold the launch till he visited the market so that they could do it with traditional fanfare. A disgruntled distributor in Raigarh (now in Chhattisgarh) sent this to the police, saying that HUL was encouraging hoarding. Remember this was the time of Emergency. An arrest warrant was issued and M.K. Sharma, along with Rustomjee, rushed to Raigarh court to get bail. As they were entering court, they met a lawyer who said that for a small fee he would definitely get Rustomjee bail. On being asked how he was sure, the lawyer said that when MK entered the court the judge would wink at him, proving the influence the lawyer had on the judge. Sure enough, when MK walked into the court, the judge winked at him. Collusion ascertained, MK told the lawyer that the company policy prevents direct or indirect bribes and he was sorry he wouldn't be able to hire him and proceeded to make alternative arrangements. The judge kept MK and Rustomjee waiting for hours. Sensing that the judge would not hear the case that day, thereby keeping Rustomjee in the cooler for the long Holi weekend, MK asked Rustomjee to leave the court and go to Raipur. At the end of the day the judge adjourned the hearing and asked that Rustomjee be kept in custody till the next working day, that is, three nights in jail. MK told the judge that being old, and being a heart patient, both true, Rustomjee had left for Raipur where he could get medical assistance. The furious judge immediately issued a non-bailable warrant and sent the police to Raipur to bring Rustomjee back. A despondent MK walked out of the court, only to find Rustomjee waiting for him on the road. There was no way Rustomjee would leave a young manager of the company at the mercy of a corrupt judge. Had the judge locked up MK for obstructing the law, Rustomjee was planning to present himself. MK sent Rustomjee to Pune and himself went to the Jabalpur High Court. Using HUL's credibility and their counsel's stature, rather than explain the situation in an open court, a chamber hearing was requested. The high court judge not only granted bail to

Rustomjee but after a couple of hearings even quashed the criminal complaint.

While in Jabalpur MK got to know that the company sales officer in Jabalpur had either knowingly or inadvertently tipped the distributor that Rustomjee's original letter could be misconstrued as hoarding. Peeved at him, MK didn't go to meet him at his house for dinner as was the custom in those days. Back in Mumbai after several hard days and a successful outcome, MK was surprised to find a formal reprimand letter on his desk. 'It was unacceptable,' the letter said, 'for a covenanted manager not to visit a salesperson when in his town.' The reprimand letter, one of two he received in his career, was on MK's confidential file till he retired.

This wonderful story reveals many facets of HUL covered in the book. The **entrepreneurial drive** for **profitability** in launching Lux Supreme when faced with price controls. The deep belief in salience-led **marketing** even among field sales managers. The **sales system's commitment** to giving it the best in the market by the manager being present for the launch in a small town like Raigarh. **Integrity** as evinced by the refusal to pay what could easily have been called a small lawyer's fee in the account book. The **courage** and **presence of mind** of a junior company lawyer in taking a risk with the law by asking the sales manager to decamp. The **caring** showed by a veteran towards a younger manager. The ability of HUL, built by its **reputation,** to move mountains to get a special hearing of a case. The simple **middle-class value** of having a meal at a salesperson's house if you visit his town. The **HR systems** that picked up a policy violation and sent a reprimand notice immediately.

I can't think of many companies that would have exhibited many of the traits mentioned above. A few perhaps would have done some. But there is one in this story that only HUL could have done. Reprimanding a successful outcome, because it involved what in hindsight was an incredibly small transgression – not having dinner at the Jabalpur salesperson's house. But that is how HUL works. This is what makes it a great company and a CEO Factory, and much, much more importantly a good one.

Acknowledgements

This short book has taken me four months to type and twenty years to write. So there's a fair bit of thanking to do.

I must first thank the wonderful brands I have worked intimately with and learnt from all these years. As St Bernard of Clairvaux said, 'You will learn more from the rocks and trees than from the masters.' Fair & Lovely, Pepsodent, Clinic Plus, Ponds, Kissan, Dalda, Annapoorna, Lux, Lifebuoy, Dove, Pears, Breeze, Surf Excel, Rin, Vim, Wheel, Brooke Bond, Taj Mahal, Taaza, Bru, Kwality Wall's, Knorr and, most recently, Horlicks and Boost.

But one also learns from the masters. My bosses Tarun Kochhar, Milind Pant, Sandeep Kataria, Sanjay Behl, Siddharth Singh, D. Chandran, Rosalind Walker, James Frost, Rohit Jawa, Gopal Vittal, Hemant Bakshi, Kevin Havelock, Winfried Hopf, Mick van Ettinger, Nitin

Acknowledgements

Paranjpe, Sanjiv Mehta and Hanneke Faber. From sixteen I have learnt how to be, and from one how not to be.

Three teams I have worked with in the past that have left an indelible impression on me: Madhya Pradesh West Sales Team (2000–02), Laundry (2008–10) and Soaps (2010–13). You are occasionally in my thoughts but often in my dreams. My wonderful current team, Foods and Refreshments, who are in my thoughts all the time now and will surely remain in my dreams when I move on to my next assignment.

In helping me convert these experiences into a book, I owe thanks to many.

Chiki Sarkar, my publisher, who along with giving me the idea of writing this book also gave me an idea to turn around one of our brands. She is the best marketeer Hindustan Unilever never had.

It is rare for a company to let a serving manager write a book about it, even rarer to allow the employee to be publicly critical. I have to specially thank HUL's chairman, Sanjiv Mehta, for his generosity in not just allowing but also encouraging me to write this book.

I wrote about half this book in an intense frenzy, during a very wet week at my farm near Kashid beach, south of Mumbai. My major-domo, Santosh Mali, regularly plied me with gin, tonic and hot bhel, all of which contributed enormously to opening up my sinus blocks, so to say. Our

238

nanny, Mary Chettiar, who – except on one occasion – kept the kids from shutting the computer before I saved an hour's work.

I am fortunate to have several talented writers and editors in the family. My wife, Ketki, who in the best traditions of Hindustan Unilever market research gave unerringly accurate advice (which, like a typical marketeer, I accepted only later, when others told me the same!) on paragraphs that should be kept and those that should be dumped. I thank my brother, Vinay Sitapati, an author himself, for never missing the wood for the trees and keeping me true to the big picture; my sister-in-law Aditi, also a writer, for turning the pedantic into finer sentences.

My mother, Kamala Ganesh, ever-meticulous about choice of words, tamed wild sentences from running amok. When I wrote somewhere 'It is wise to crystallize this moment in a bottle and constantly take swigs from it' she wrote in the margins 'You can't take swigs from crystals in a bottle. Maybe "condense" or "distil"?'

Several friends and colleagues, well chosen for their straight talk, were given the manuscript and asked to be brutal in their feedback. They more than lived up to their brief. Vivek Trilokinath, Shubhranshu Singh, Prasad Pradhan, Dev Bajpai, Satyam Vishwanathan, Jayadev Calamur, Sajith Pai, Swati Apte, Anandi Shankar, Anant Rangaswami and Priya Krishnan. Priya spent many hours making this book more readable, making me realize that what I learnt in B-school, I lost in terms of grammar and syntax.

Despite this strict editing, the mistakes were so many that it took an editor of the calibre of Jaishree Ram Mohan to catch what had escaped through the filter.

Sayan Bhattacharya has done a lot of grunge work fact-checking for the book. Piyush Sharma helped me craft an online study to test various title options for the book and Beena Parekh helped design a lovely cover which sadly flunked Piyush's test. Zubin Bhathena has as usual been more instrumental in the publication of this book than he realizes. Saikiran Krishnamurthy and M.G. Subrahmanyam helped me get recommendations for the book.

Several colleagues and former colleagues generously helped me with the anecdotes that pepper the book. I have acknowledged them through the book but without naming them individually. I want to thank them here for it. In particular, three members of HUL's current management committee – Srinandan Sundaram, Pradeep Banerjee and Anuradha Razdan – helped me structure the chapters on sales, costs and HR.

If it takes a village to raise a child, it takes somewhat more than that to turn a soap salesperson into an author. There are several people who may not have directly contributed, but who have influenced my thinking in some form or other. I doubt that I could have written this book without them:

T.S.R. Subramanian, Ramanathan 'Tennis' Krishnan, Ramesh Krishnan, R. Srinivasan, A.V. Krishnan, R. Krishnan, Bhaskara Mannar Marthi, Vijaya Venkatesh Mannar, Sangram Gaikwad, Bala Govindan, E. Sendil, Ustad Abdul Halim Jaffer Khan, Professor Felix Almeida, Professor V. Krishnan, Sandeep Singhal, Ravi Ramamoorthi, Rahul Sami, Professor A.K. Jain, Mishka Sinha, P.S. Viswanathan, Rama Bijapurkar, Nishad Kapadia, Joe D'Souza, Derek Hill and John Lloyd.

The blessings of the elders in the family have been an intangible source of strength – my grandmothers, S. Padmavati and Chellam Ramanathan. Lalitha Krishnan, Lalitha Subramanian, J. Sitapati, Neela Janakiram, Shobha Krishnan, Venkatesh Mannar, Uma Srinivasan, Vinay and Sushma Puri.

My in-laws Sushma and Kanwal Sachdev have spent a large part of their retired life looking after our kids, so we can work and, in the little free time that is left, write books. This book would not have been possible without them.

Finally, to the three children, Sahaana, Siya and Kabir. I do hope they grow up and join Hindustan Unilever!

Click the QR Code with a QR scanner app
or type the link into the Internet browser
on your phone to download the app.

For our complete catalogue, visit www.juggernaut.in
To submit your book, send a synopsis and two
sample chapters to books@juggernaut.in
For all other queries, write to contact@juggernaut.in